Adult Coloring Series

I0486092

People Dreams #4

Trannies, TVs & Entertainers

by
KerryDean

Released for sale
in support of the RocketHub Project:
http://bit.ly/1HCuLk9

We *APPRECIATE* your creations,
and Want to Show Them
from the Online Mountain Tops!
Attach a scan of your favorite and email to:

Info@**TeamWorx-Inc**.com

A sense of humility requires us to refrain
from trumpeting our perfection, so
IF you have any feedback, criticism or praise
to share, simply let us know at:
Info@TeamWorx-Inc.com

And IF IF IF you don't like this coloring book,
we'll quickly refund your fee.

Just email us at guarantee@TeamWorx-Inc.com

These were all drawn from life, between 1985 and 1990; in Pattaya and Bangkok,
Thailand, during the artist's Toulouse Lautrec phase.

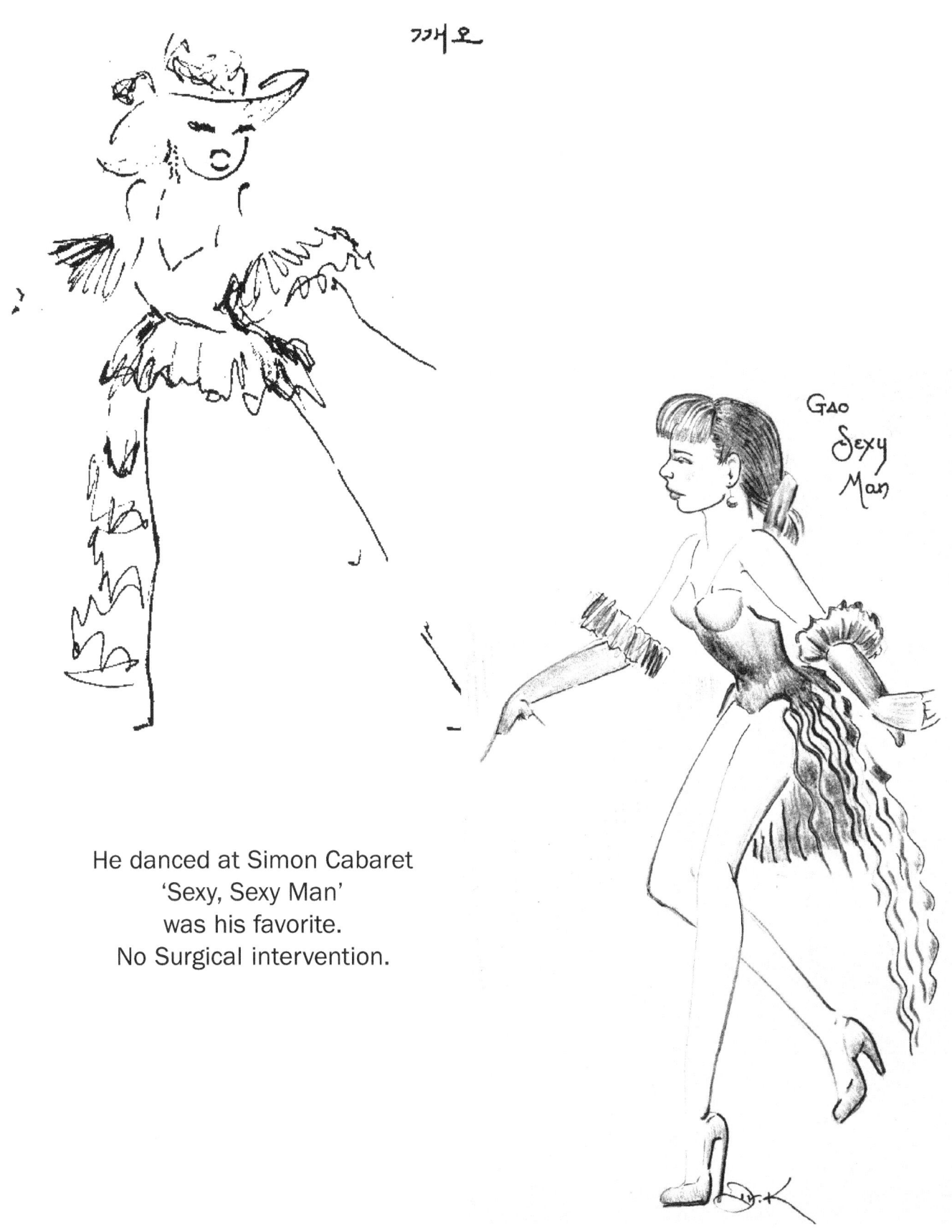

He danced at Simon Cabaret
'Sexy, Sexy Man'
was his favorite.
No Surgical intervention.

So here you are, with these line-drawings,
just waiting for YOUR artistic touch to fill in color and details.
(Then see Appendix for some stories behind the faces.)

Also from Simon Cabaret, in South Pattaya, came this lovely TS named Eung. She was young, lithe, talented and rumored to have starred in a film in Hong Kong...

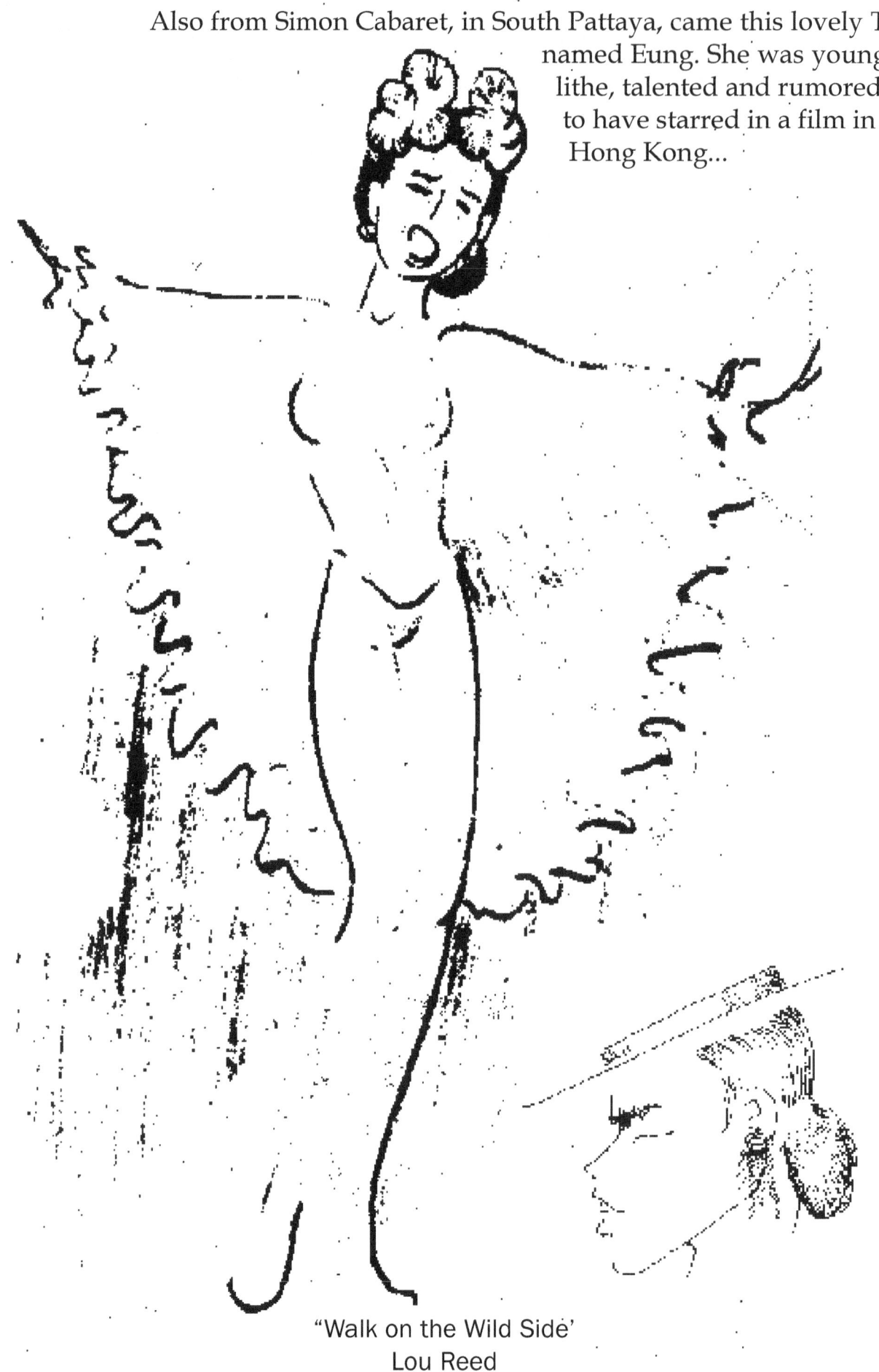

"Walk on the Wild Side'
Lou Reed

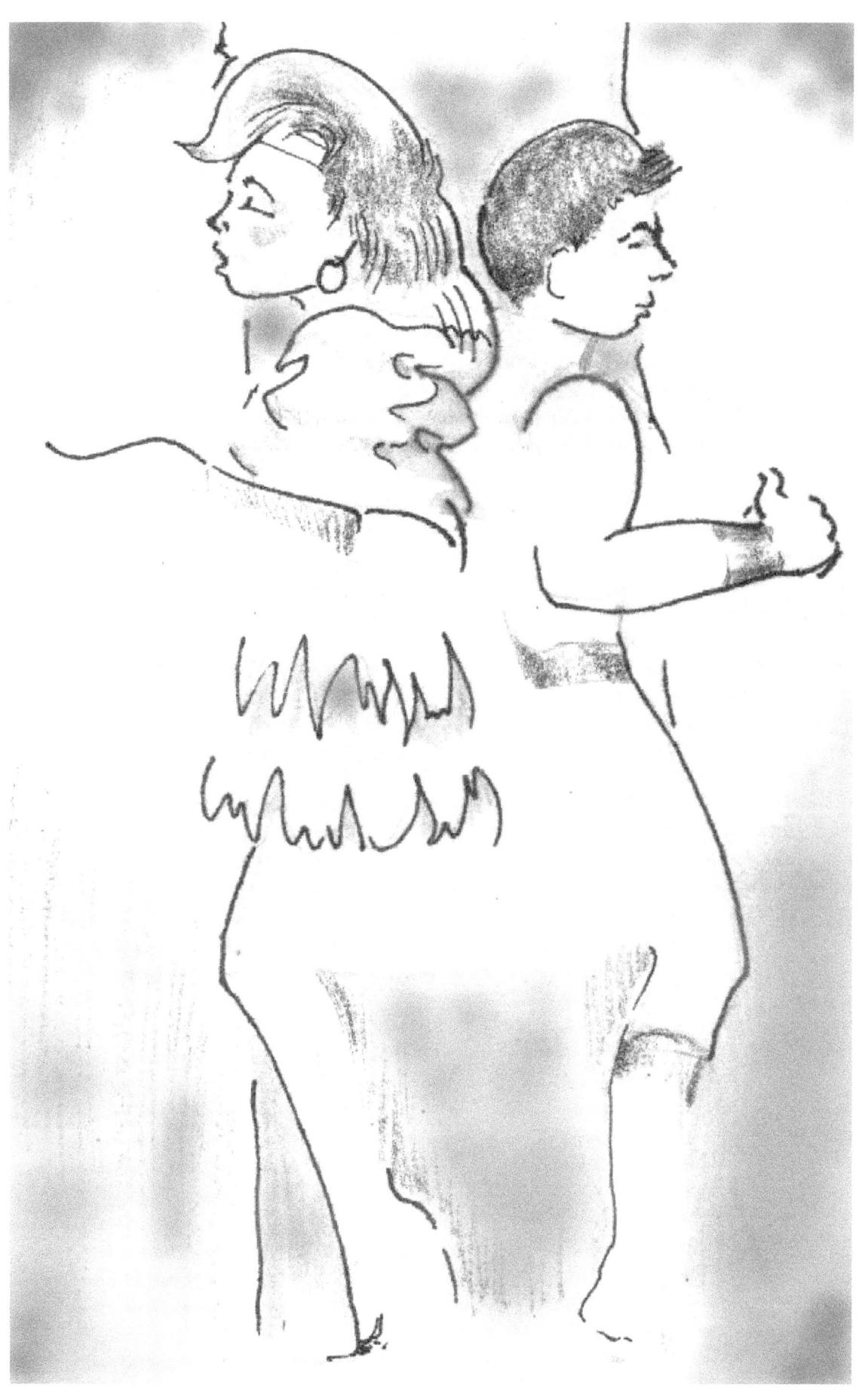

One entertainer, to 'One-Man Woman'
by Paul Anka.

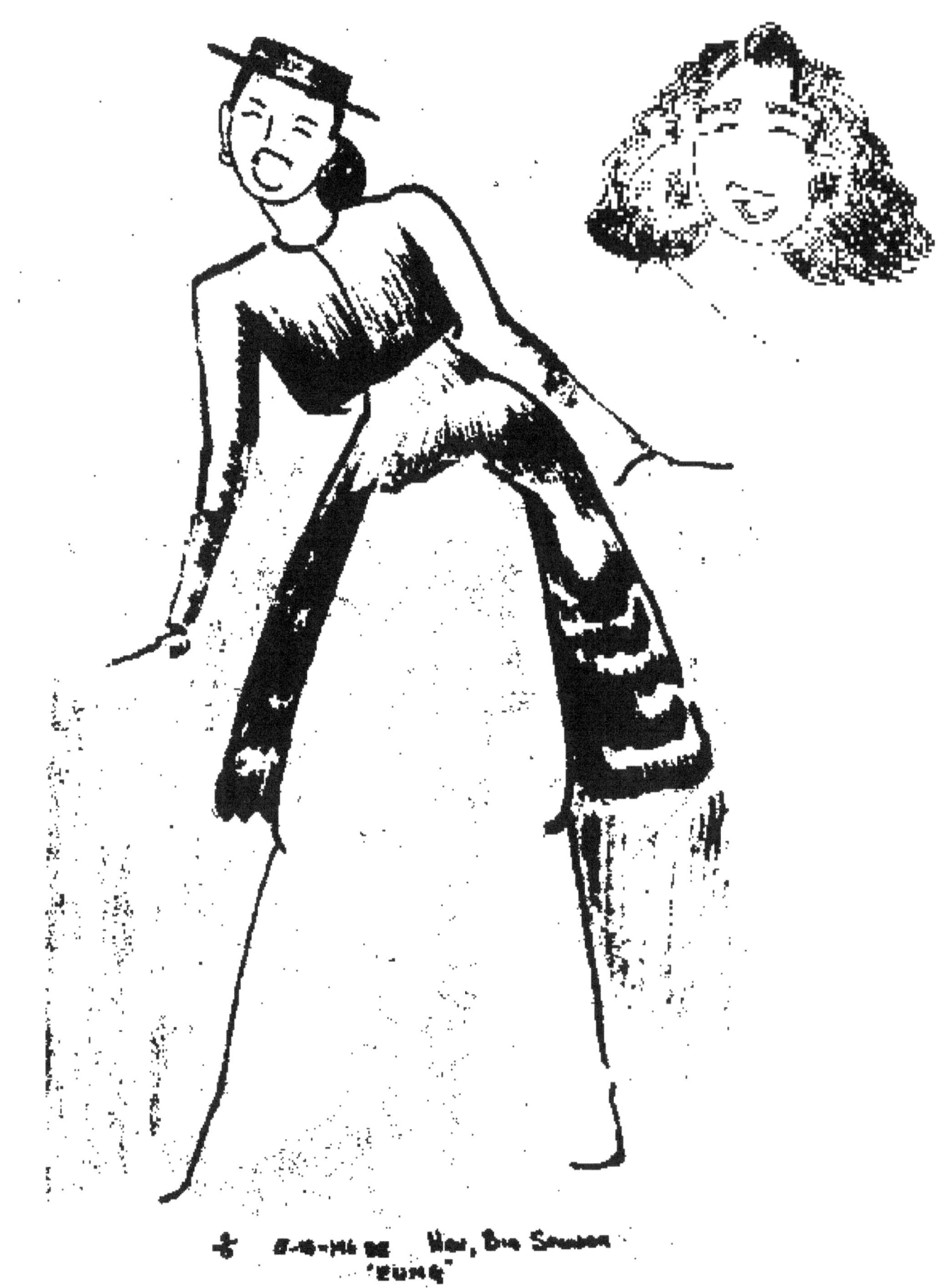

Eung, from Simon Cabaret, in a green & black outfit!

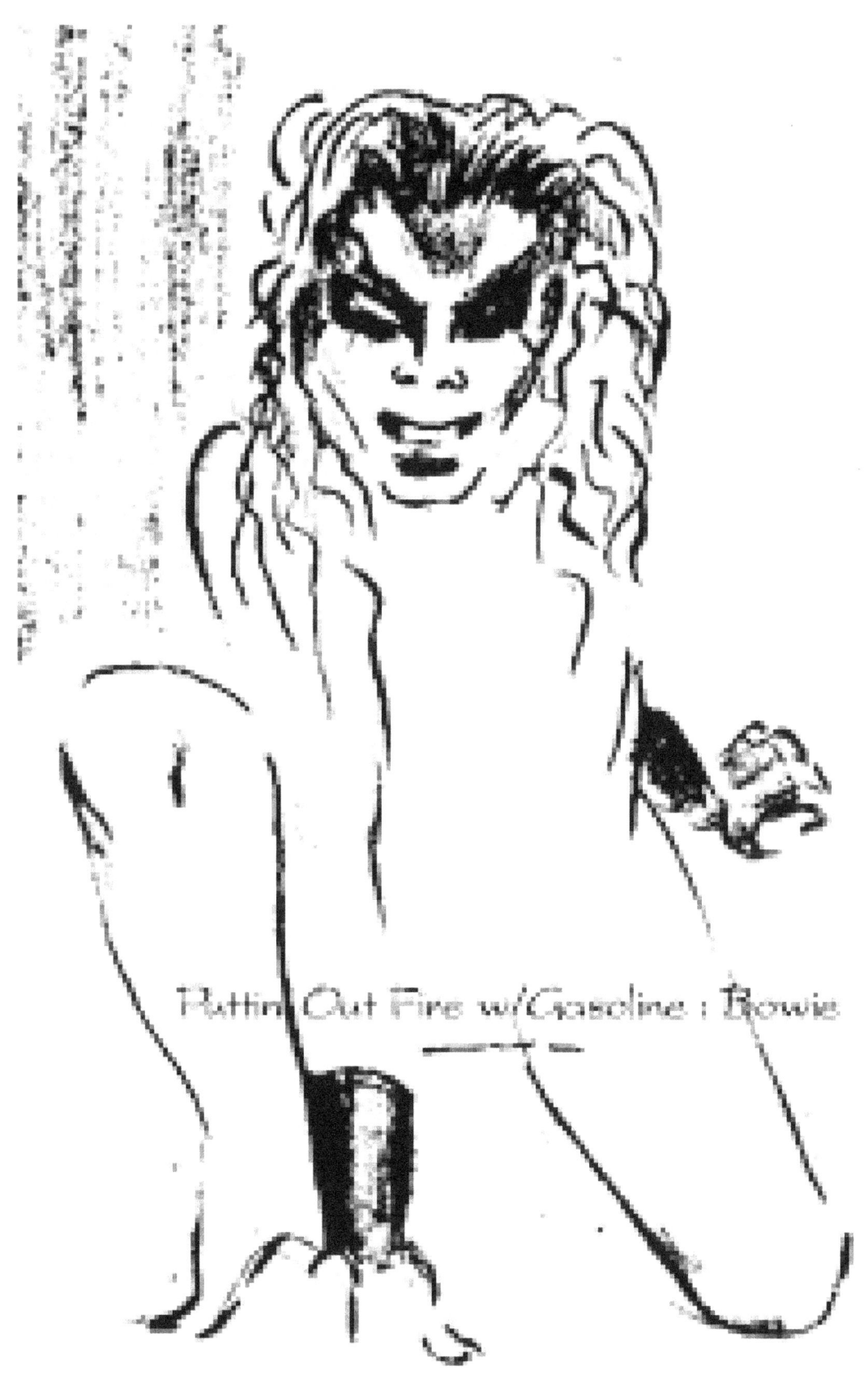

Sam, a manly guy, 'Puttin' Out Fire With Gasoline'
by **David Bowie**

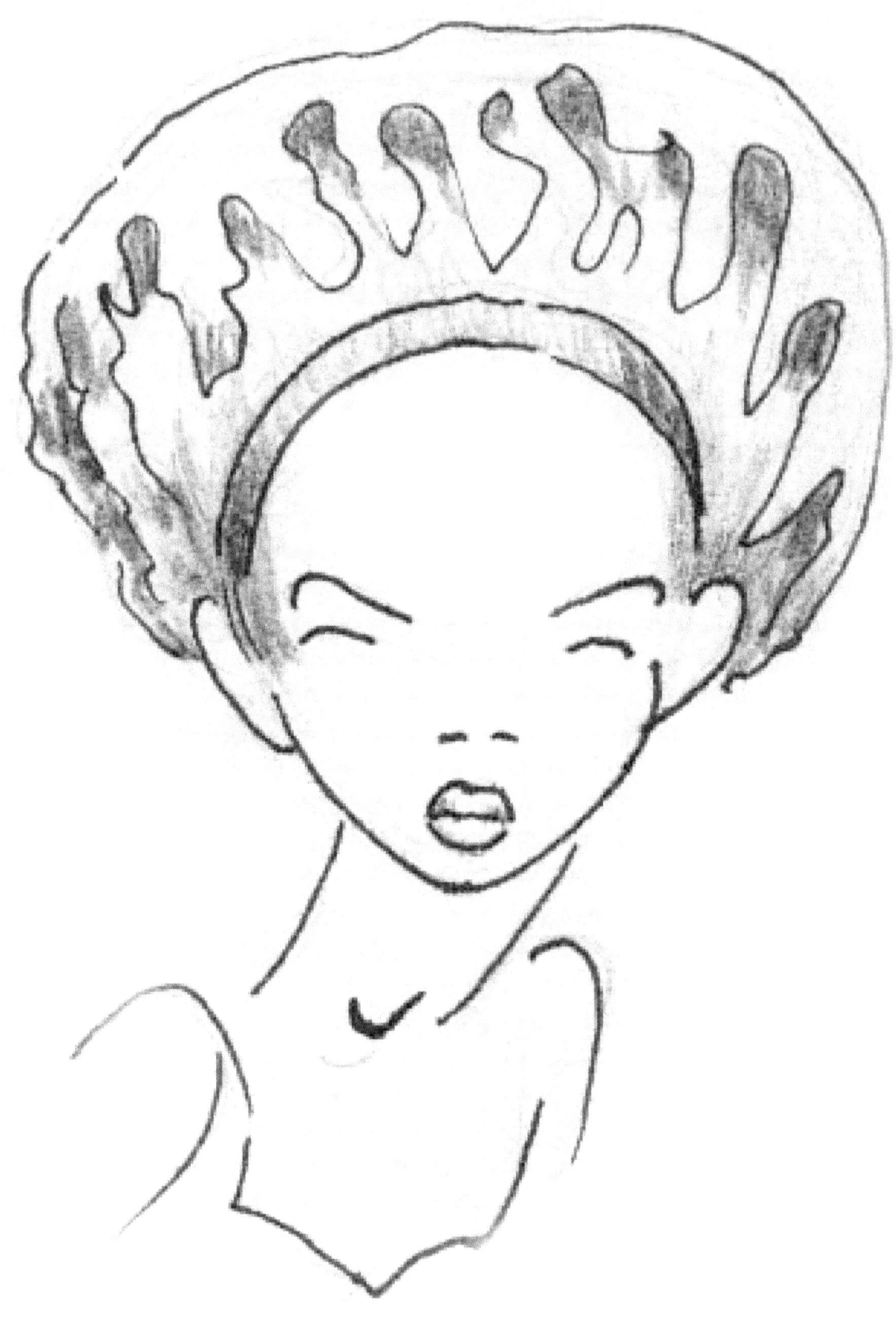

This, and next page, came from the 'Boy's Town section of South Pattaya.

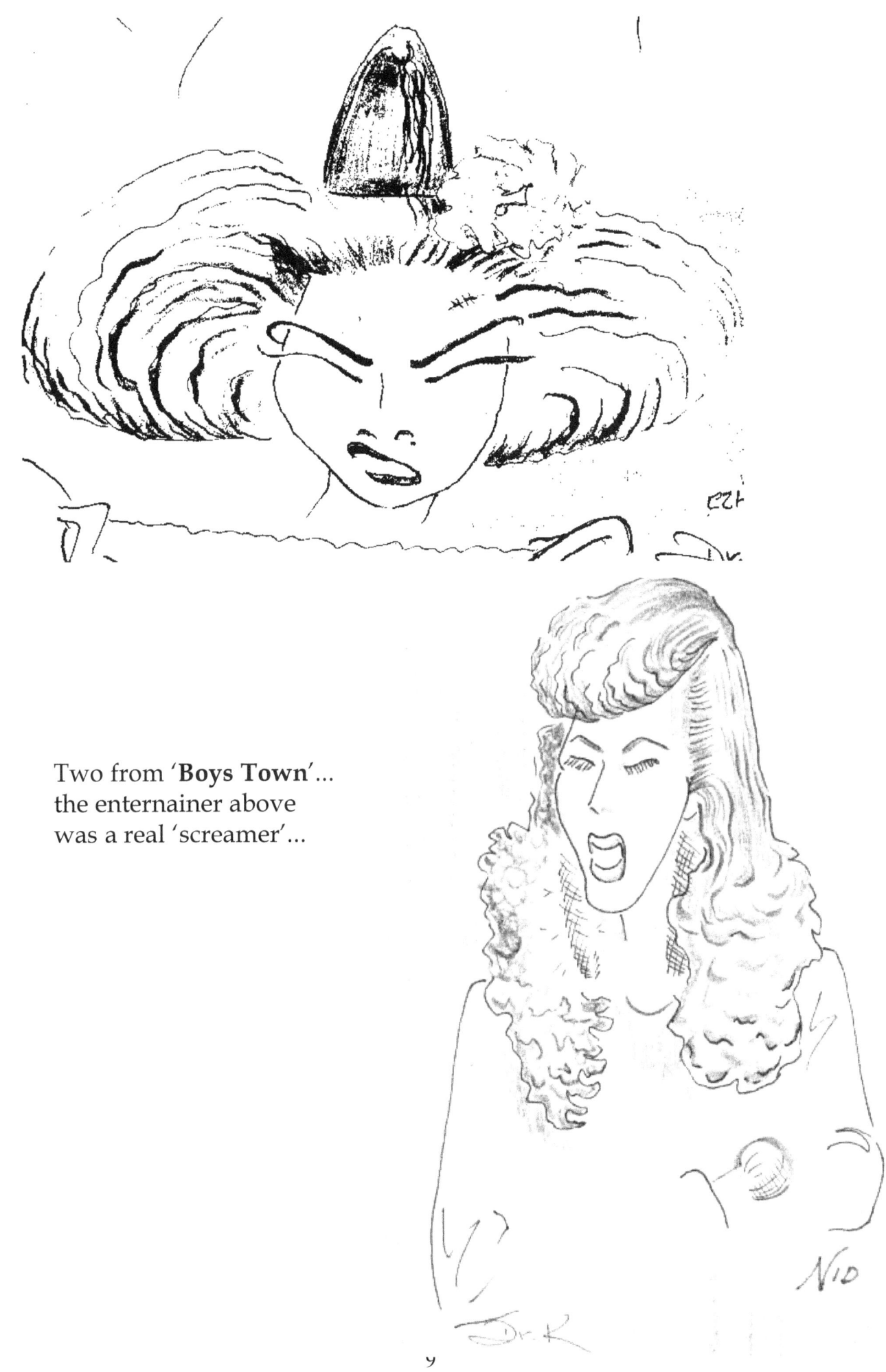

Two from '**Boys Town**'...
the enternainer above
was a real 'screamer'...

1. Use colored pencils, water-soluble is best, because when you've finished pencil-coloring, you can -*if you want to*- go back with a fine water-color paint-brush with water-damp only and play with slowly merging various patches and colors...

2. Turn off your desktop, your phone, tablet, pad and tin-can speaker-phones, so you have some actual QUIET for a few moments...

3. Go to your favorite page and start there. Go from lighter colors to darker, so you avoid muddy, brown-black finished pictures, but other than this... *anything goes!*

4. Begin coloring. Note how different strokes give you different textures. Experiment. Play! Pencil point size and shape also affect your picture. Up to down? Down to up? Diagonal? Fine point? Wedge-shaped? Blunt?

5. You may note after a few moments, that you're focusing on colors, light, shapes, hope, life, justice, courtesy and a host of other GOOD FEELINGS. *Enjoy*. These are your normal, natural birthright feelings, and you have every right to feel this way. When you notice you feel more creative, content, imaginative, playful or excited, REJOICE! You deserve these feelings!

Remember that coloring here, like writing a love-letter or making acoustic music or singing in a choir or growing in love, IS the payoff of the exercize and needs no permission or rationalizing.

"Art is a human act. **Art is Risky**. Generous. Courageous. Provocative. You can be perfect, or you can make art. You can keep track of what you will get in return for your effort, or you can make art. You can enjoy the status quo, or you can **make art**."

Erik Wahl

*Some color tips from their actual in-person performances, in the Appendix.

For other Adult Coloring Books by Karridine, with original line-drawings from life, see the '*People Dreams*' series.

The Cleanup Crew Project:

RocketHub.com

http://www.rockethub.com/59614

This coloring book for adults is like many other adult coloring books that grew out of the Art Therapy movement and really became popular around 2013CE.

Created to help fund the indie film (for a possible series), this book also helps people understand some of the difficulties for people seeking racial harmony in World War II.

The **Nazi**onal Socialists (Nazis) OPENLY said that their 'white' race was a superhuman race and deserved to control, rule over and benefit from all other 'sub-humans', which included blacks, Asians, ALL-non-whites, Gypsies, Slavic, Jews, Arabic homosexual and retarded... and the list went on and on!

So '**Cleanup Crew**' pays homage to all who fought against the racist, destructive goals of the National *Socialists* and their allies.

http://www.rockethub.com/59614
Donate Today!

http://bit.ly/1HCuLk9

Find on Amazon the adult coloring book:
Cleanup Crew
for more coloring pleasure!

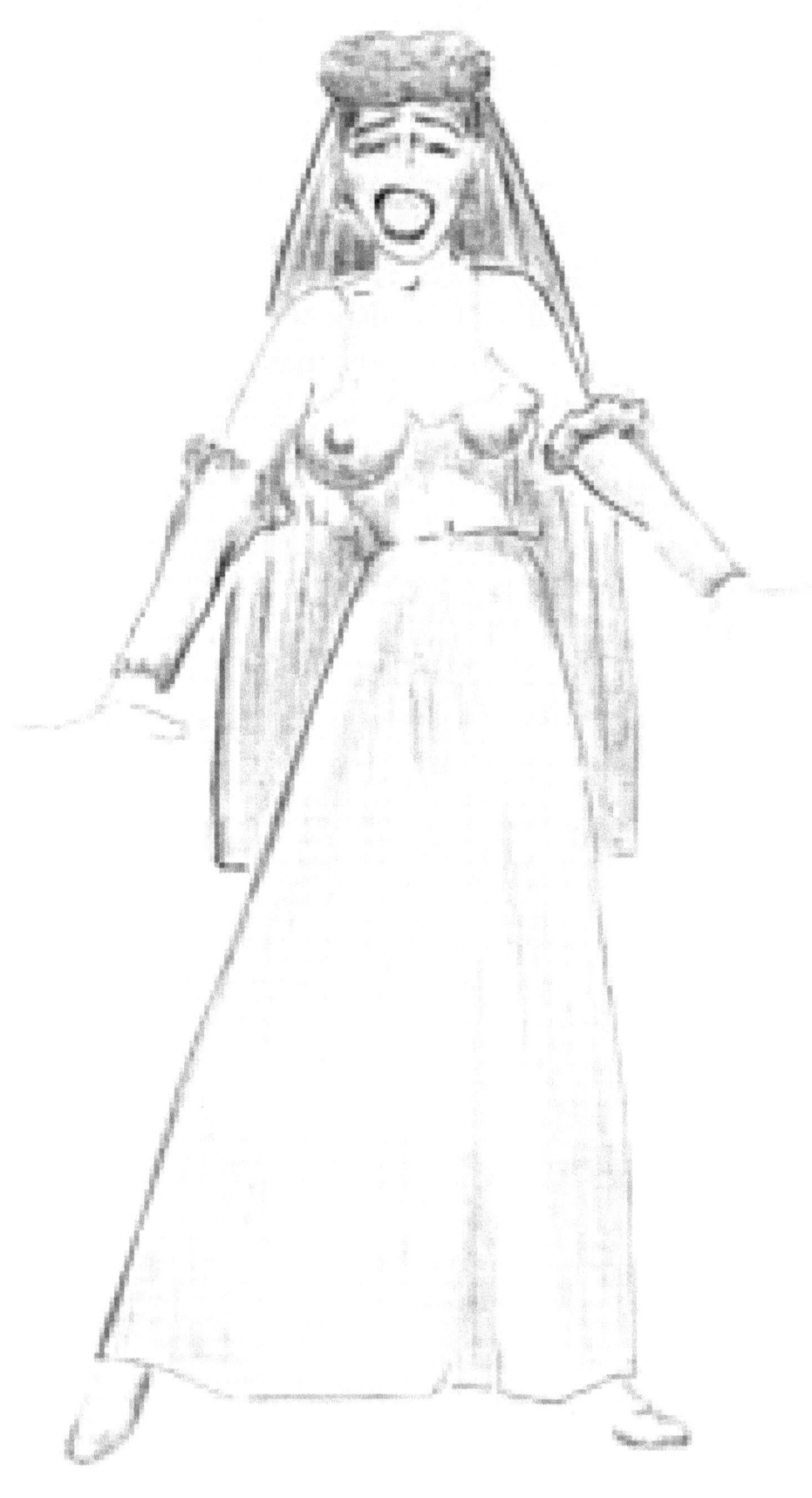

Eung's expensive physical resculpting
didn't MAKE her a star...

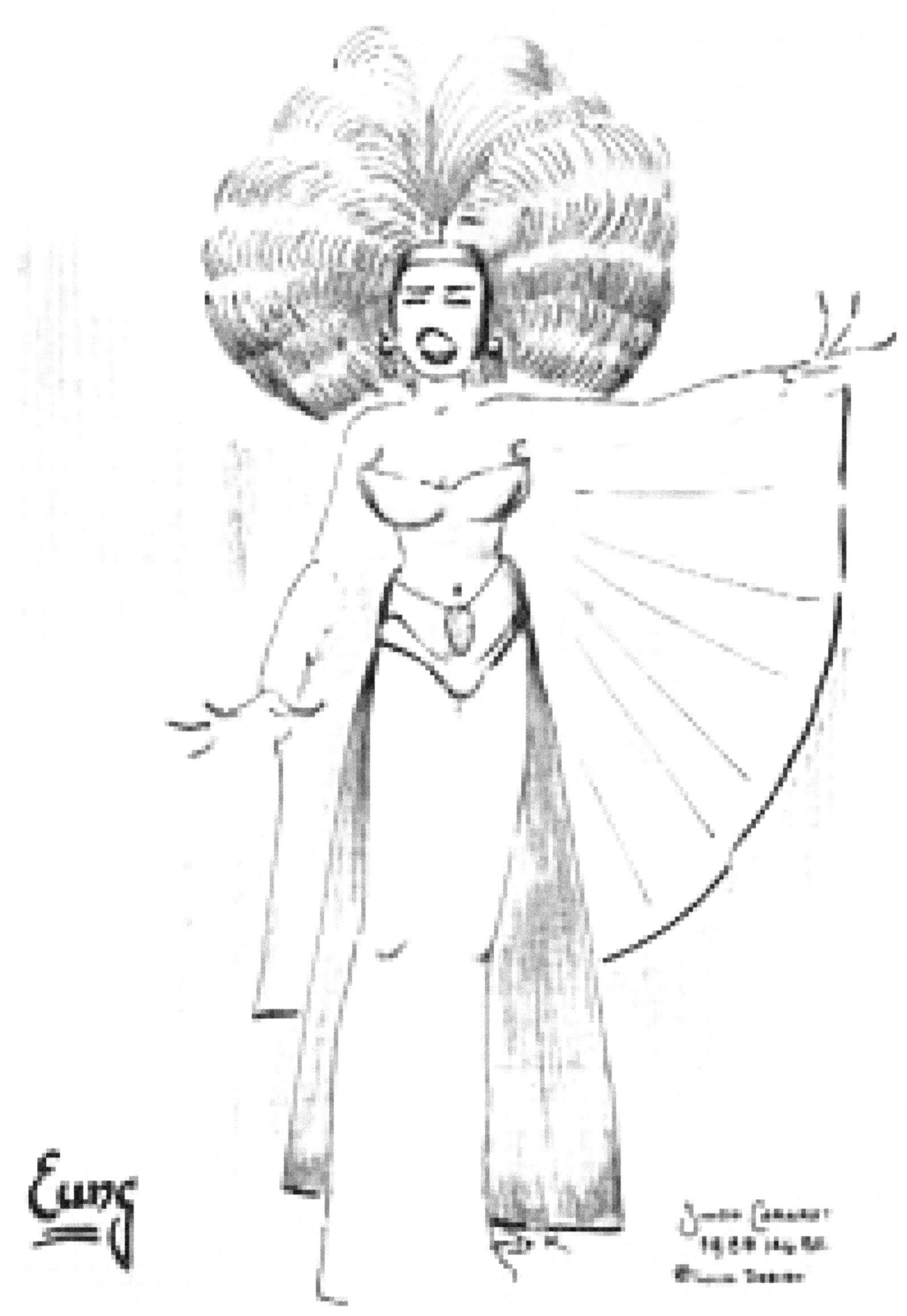

...but she made the most of it while she could!

Eung, in her reddish head-dress
and scarlet dress...

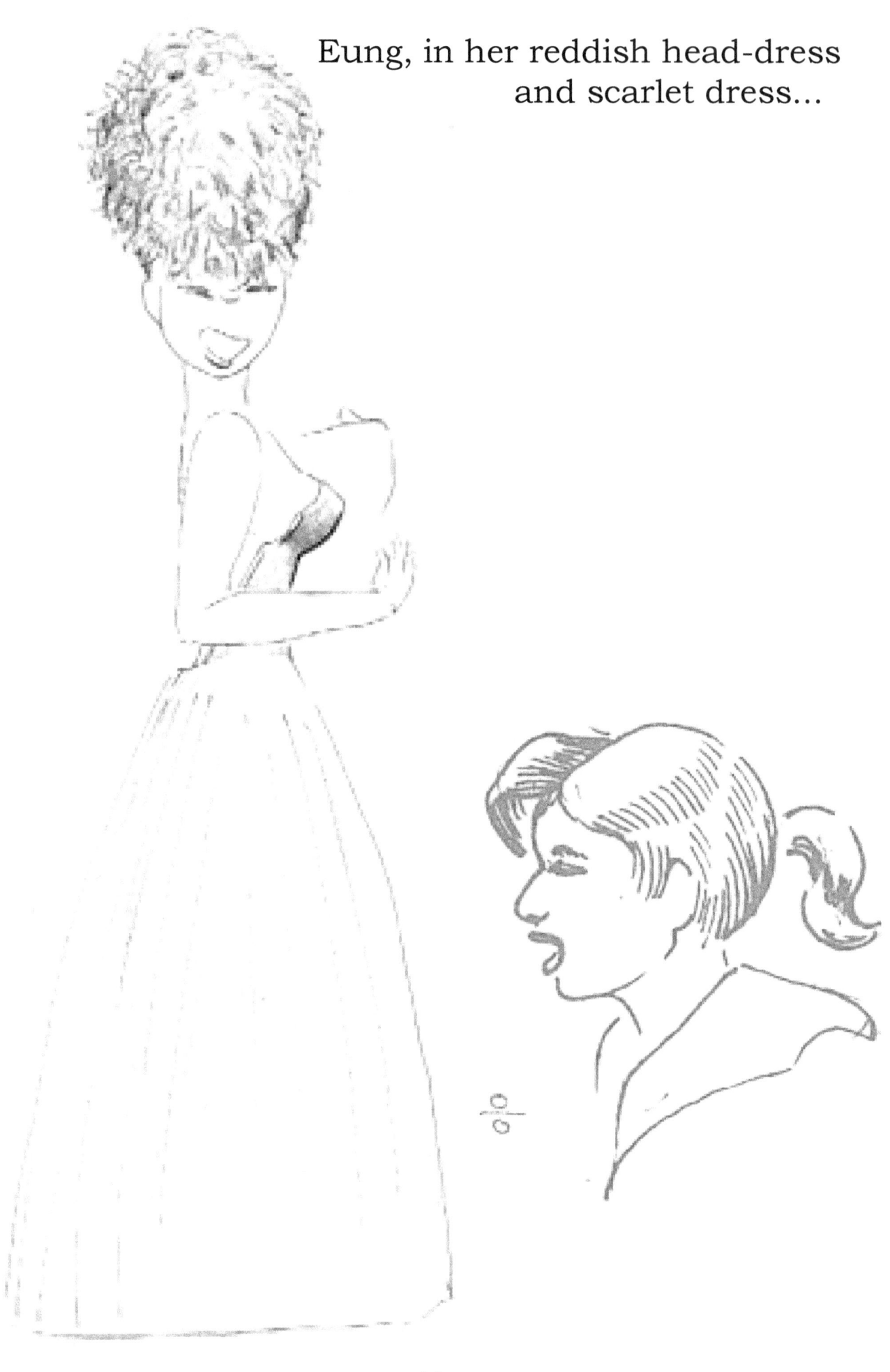

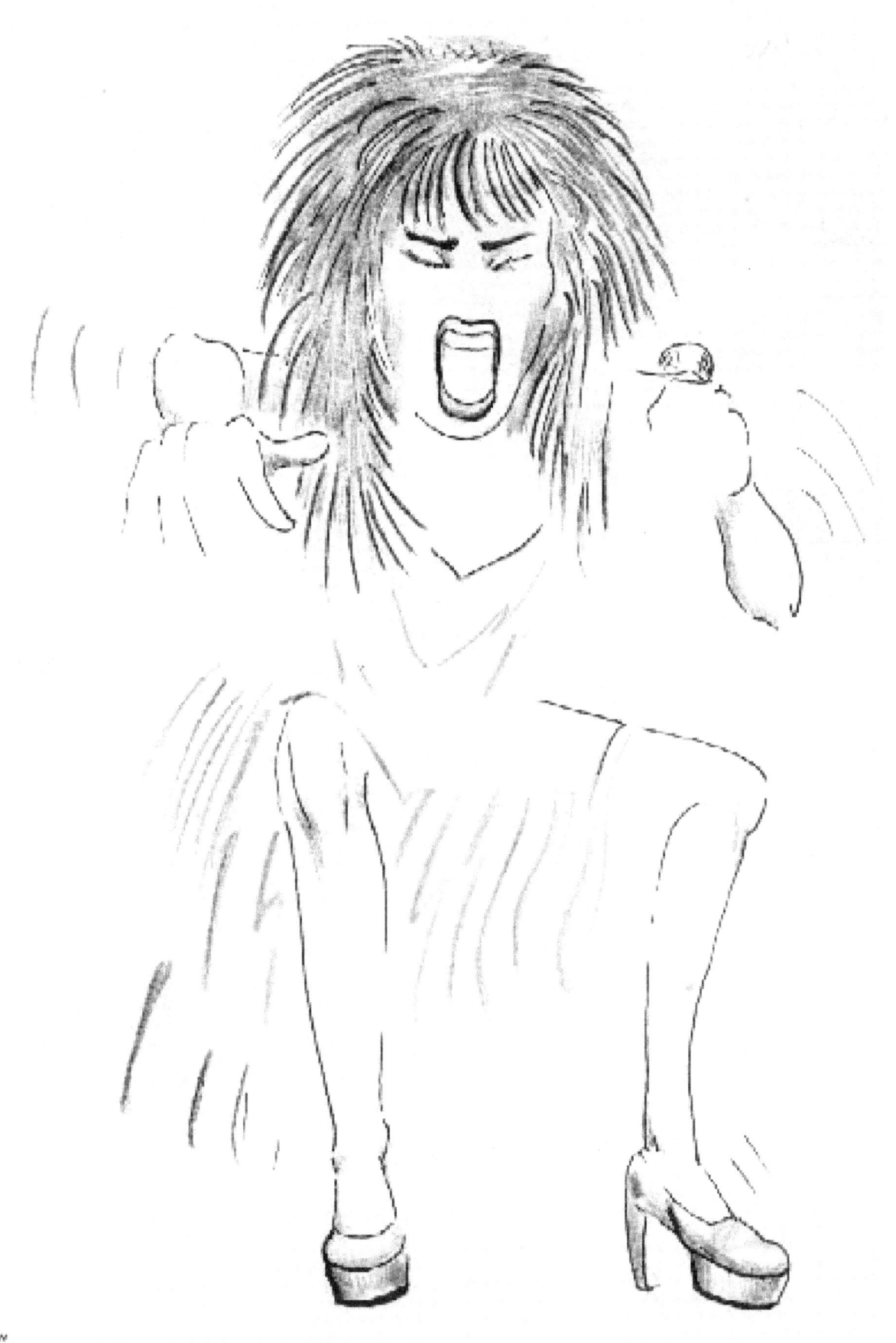

Chae, lip-synching Tina Turner!

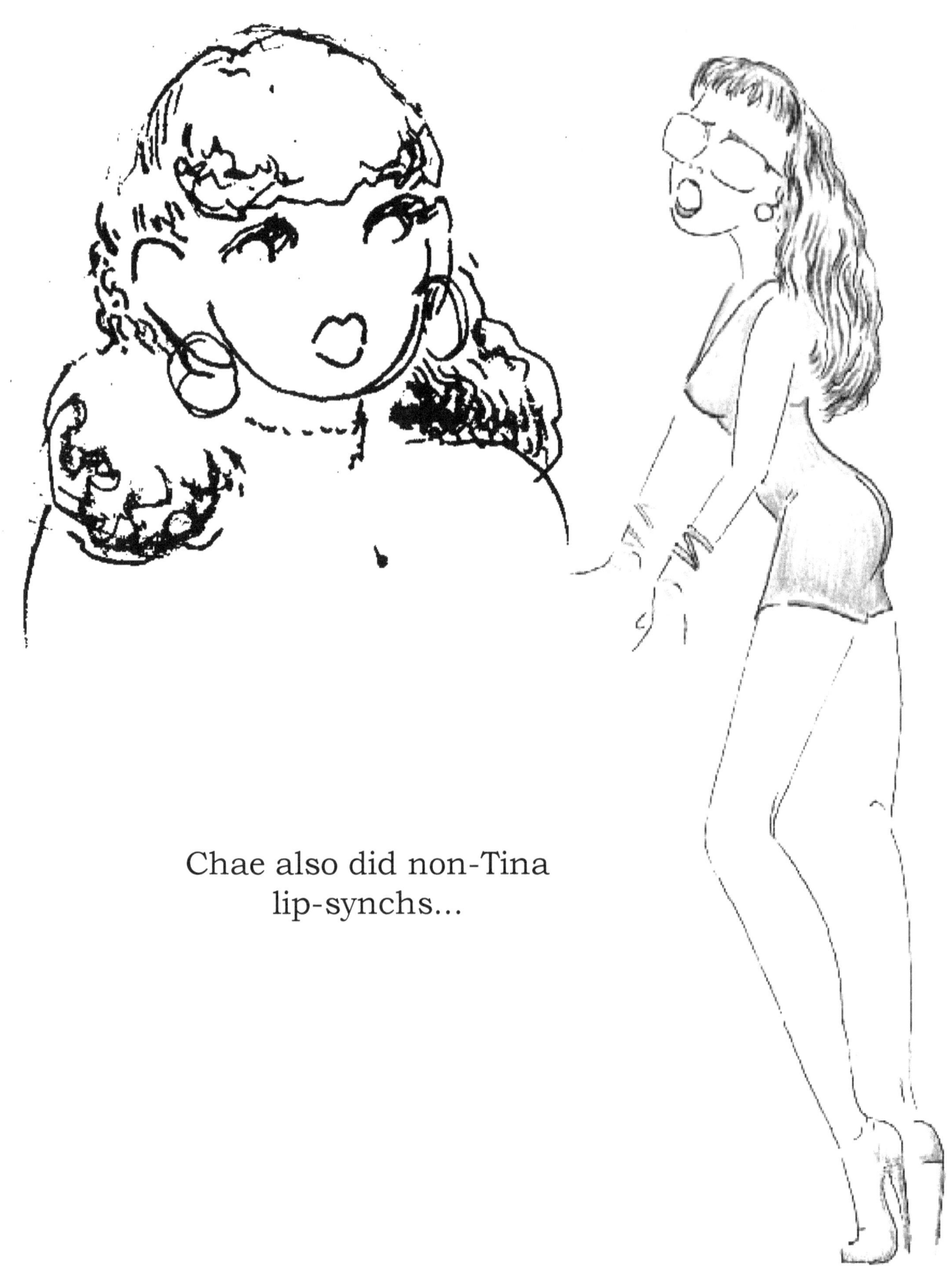

Chae also did non-Tina
lip-synchs...

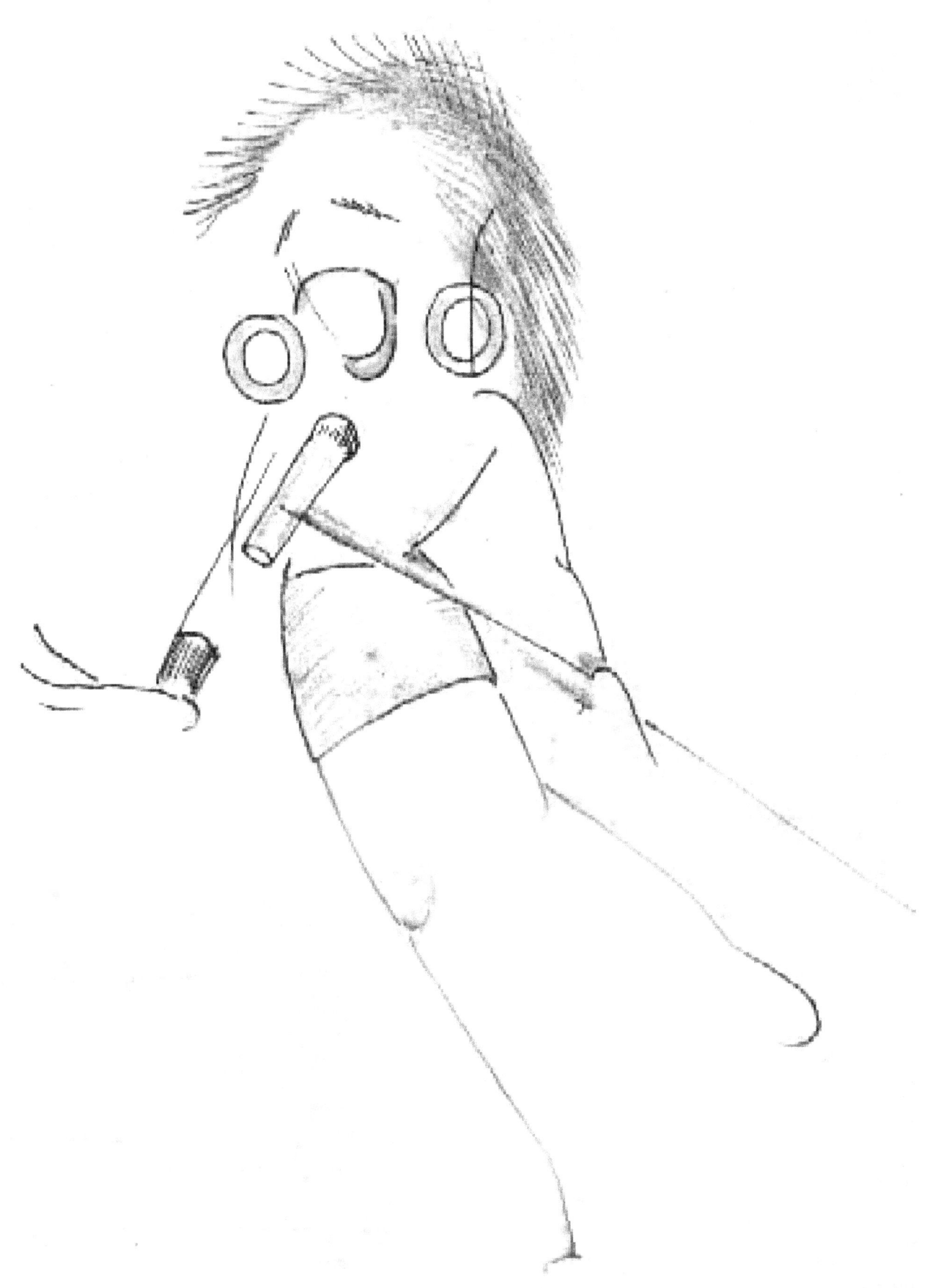

...but dang! he was popular
as Tina Turner!

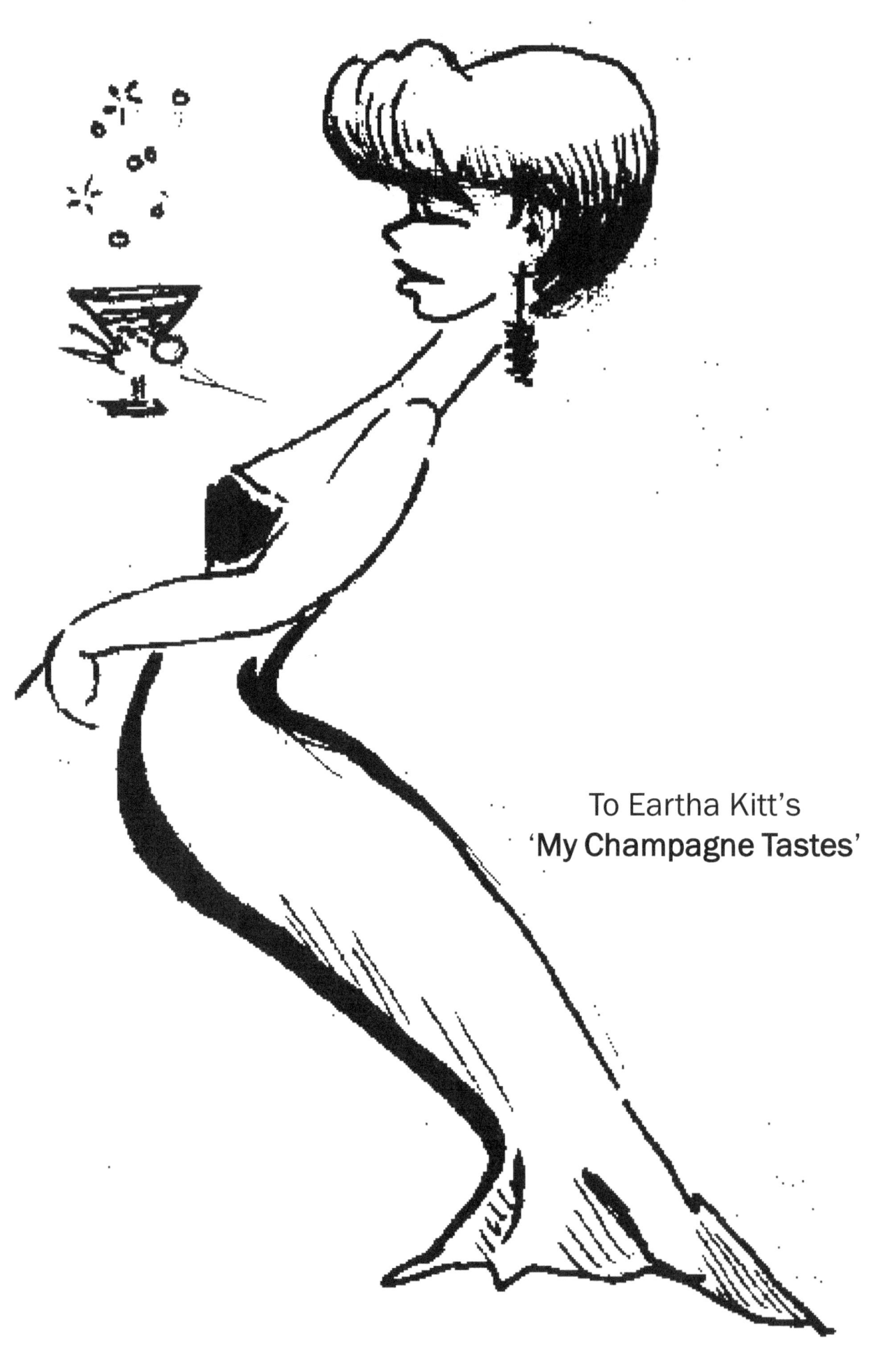

To Eartha Kitt's
'My Champagne Tastes'

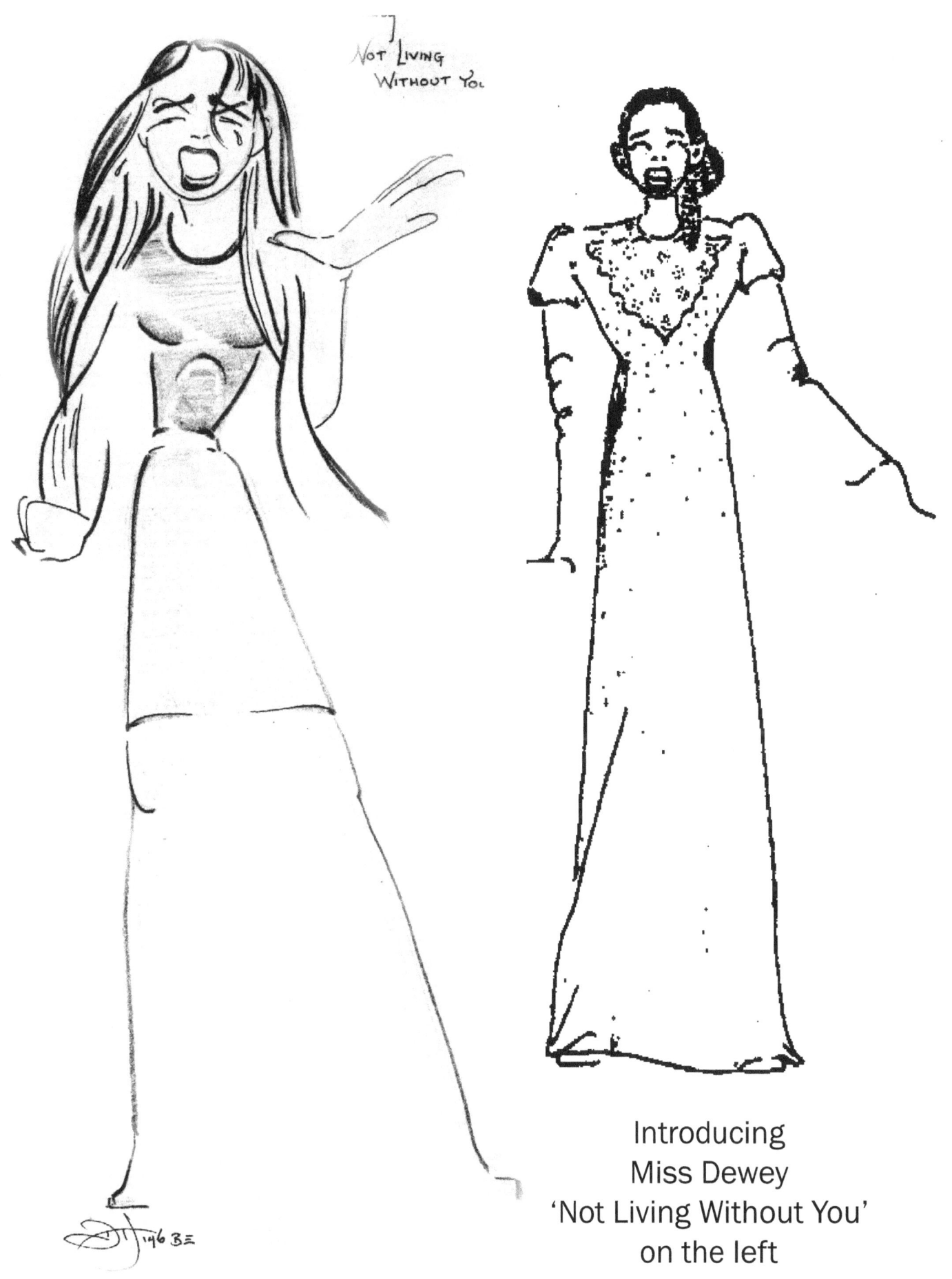

Introducing
Miss Dewey
'Not Living Without You'
on the left

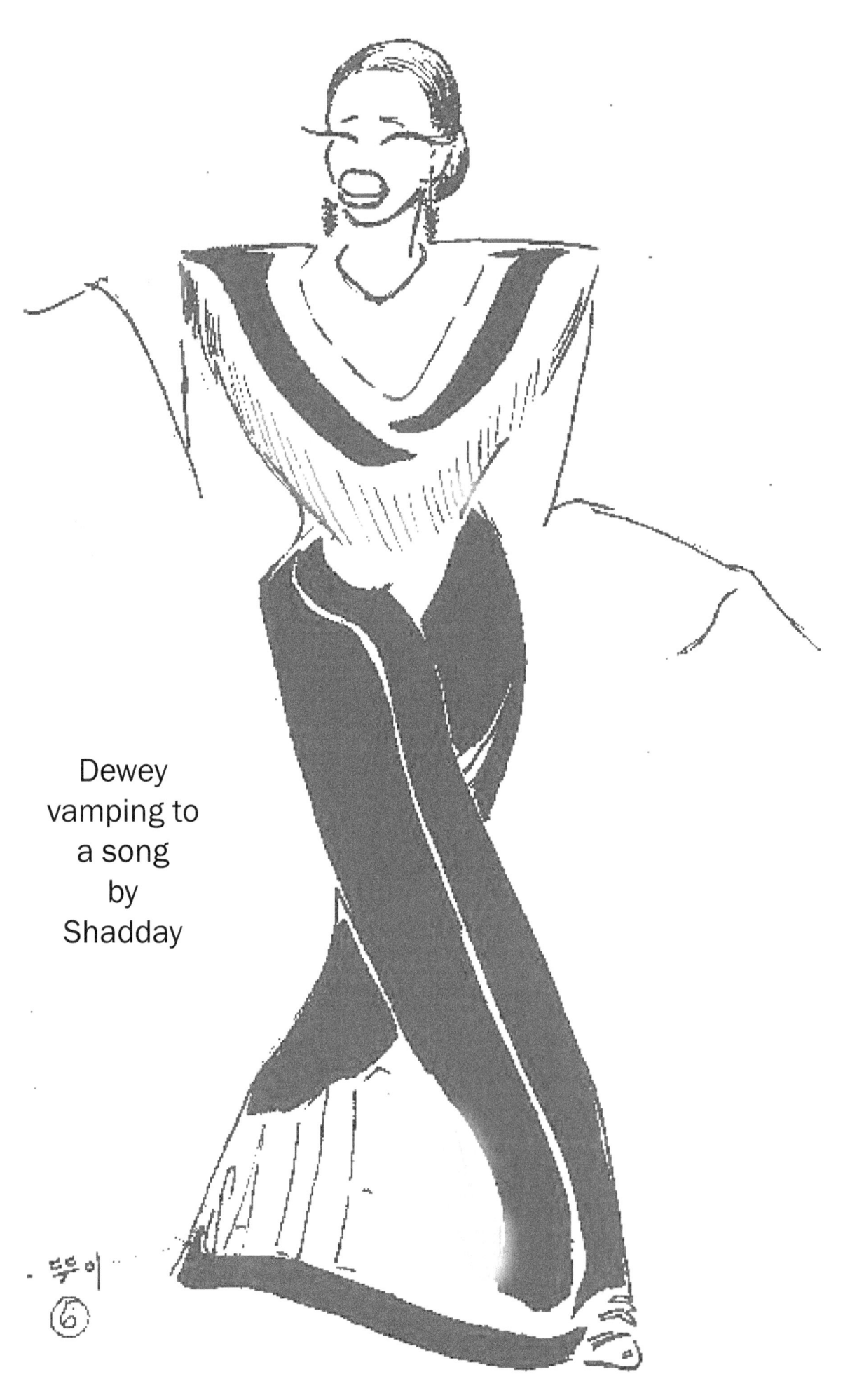

Dewey
vamping to
a song
by
Shadday

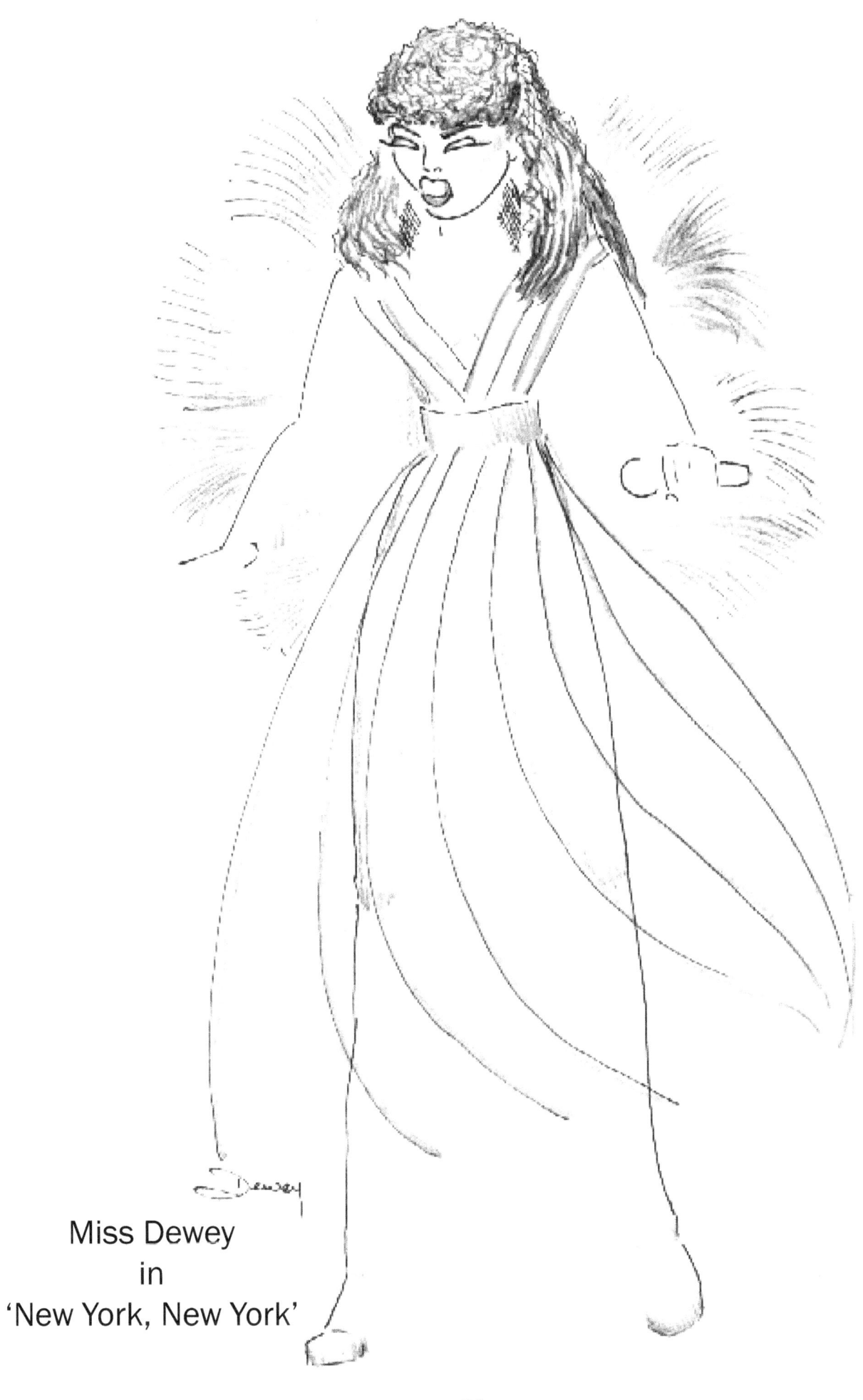

Miss Dewey
in
'New York, New York'

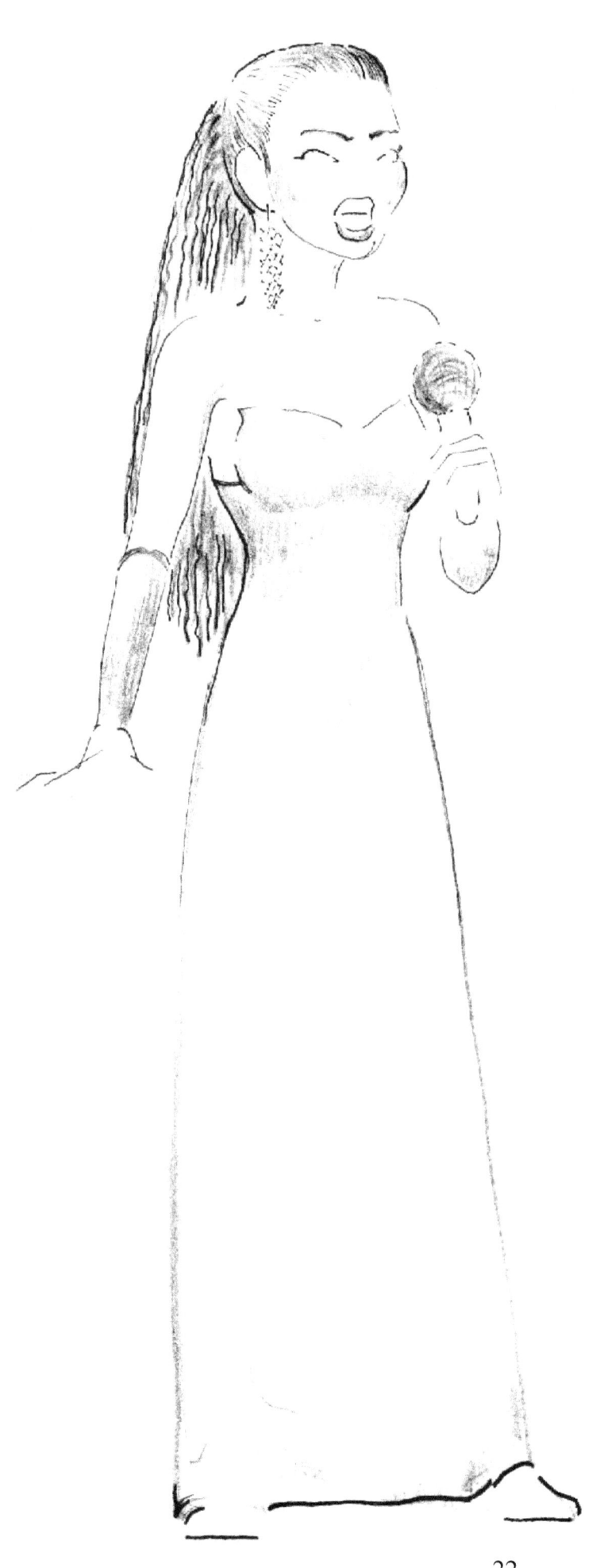

Dewey
in her
silver-blue gown

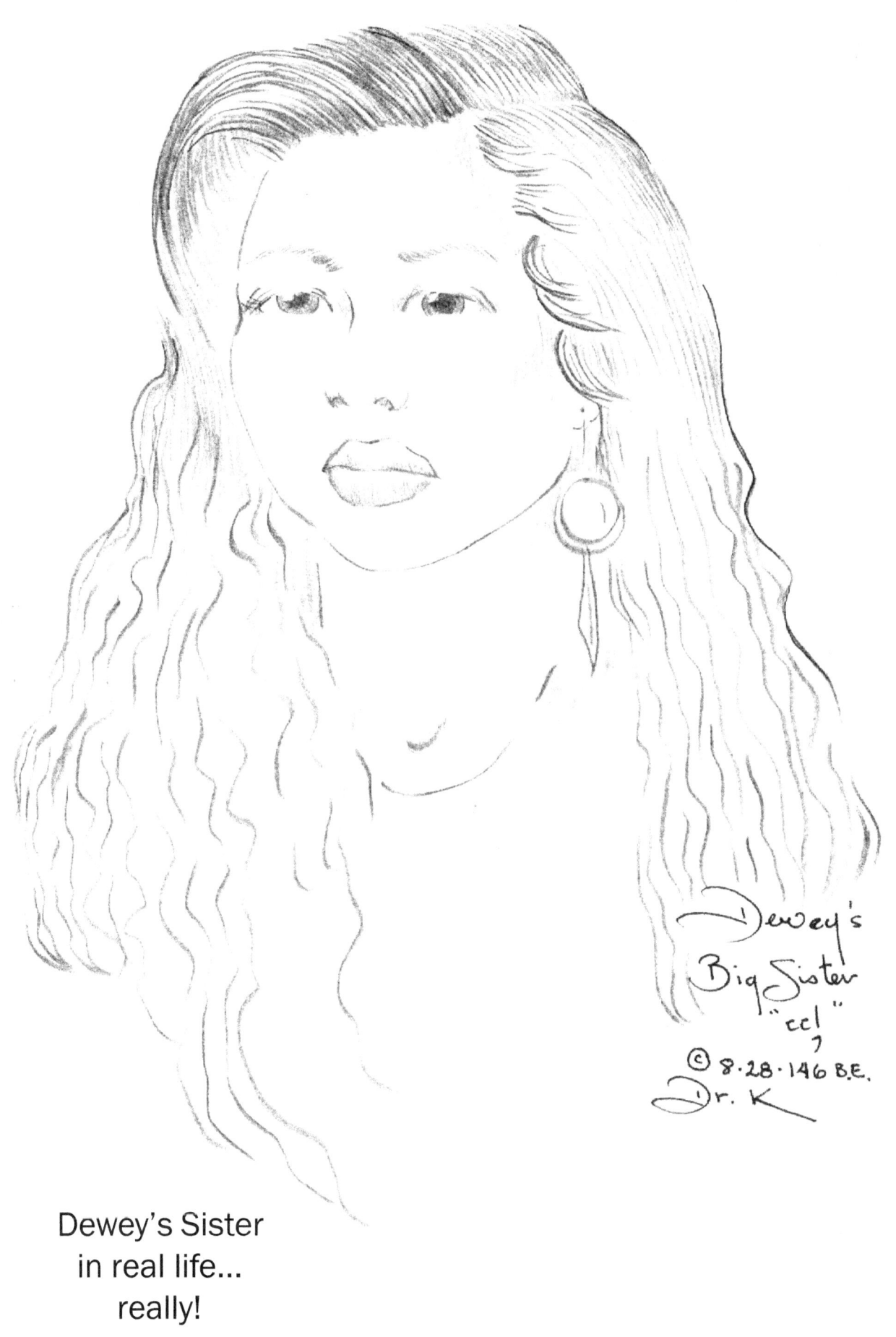

Dewey's
Big Sister
"ccl"
© 8·28·146 B.E.
Dr. K

Dewey's Sister
in real life...
really!

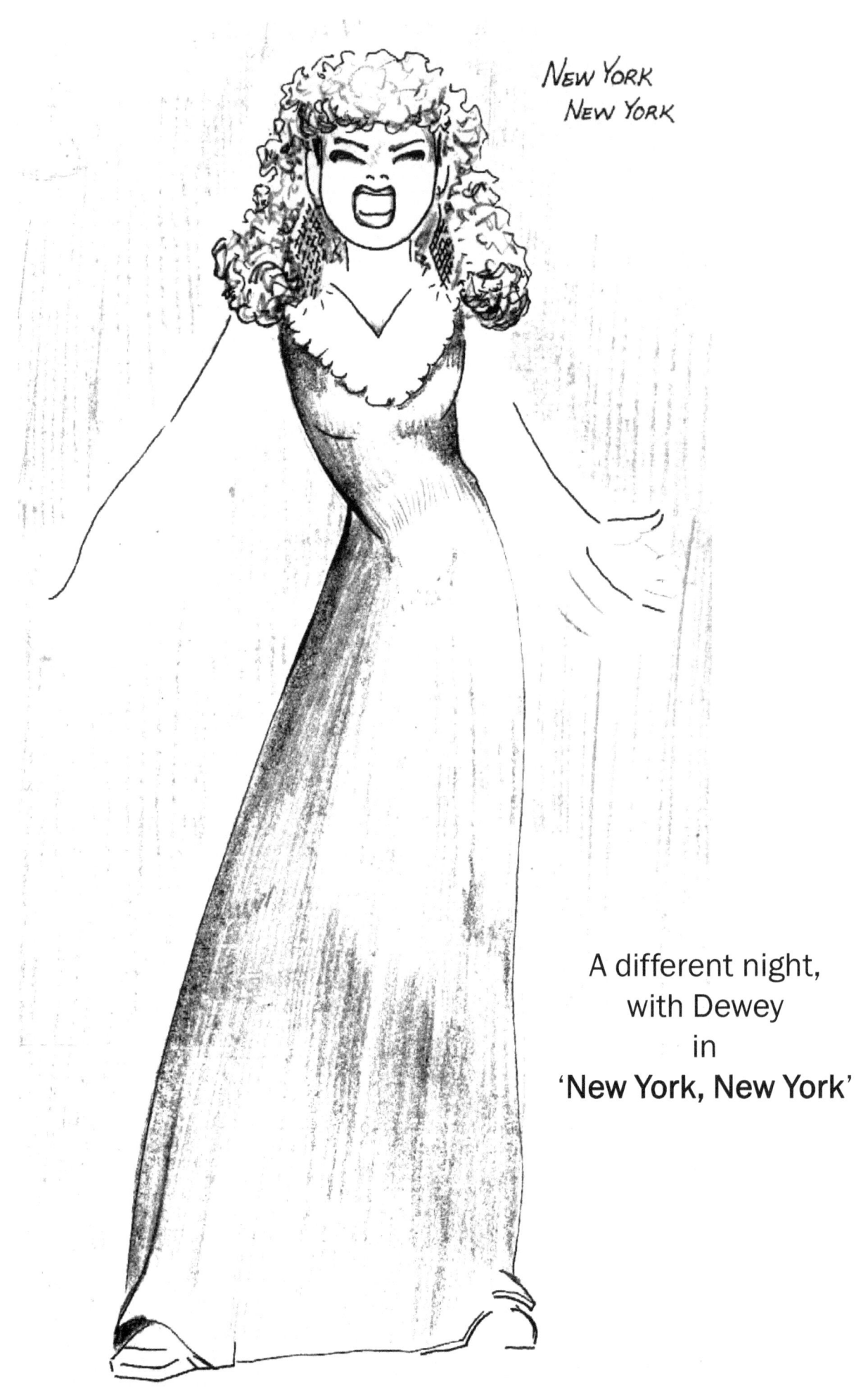

NEW YORK
NEW YORK

A different night,
with Dewey
in
'New York, New York'

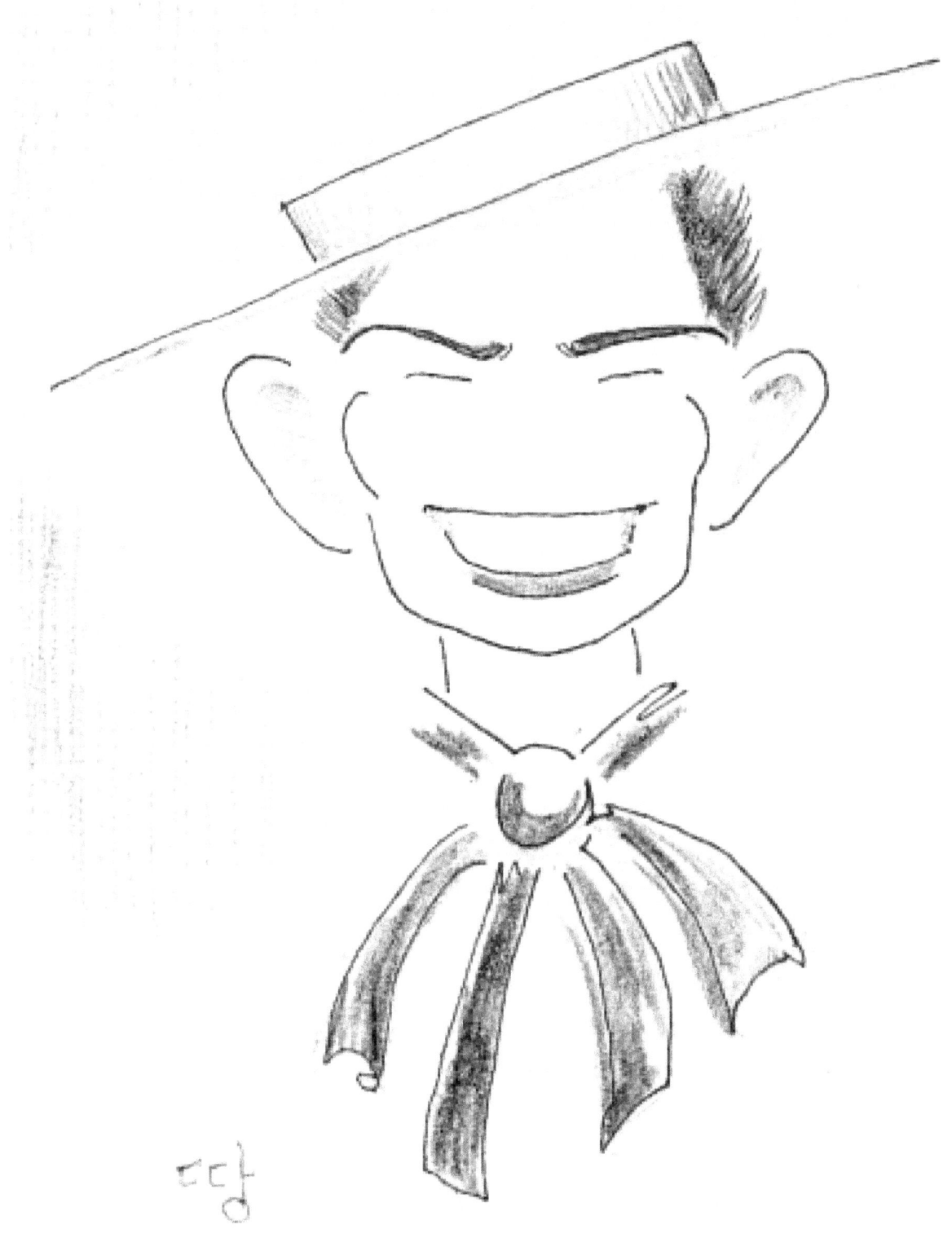

A smiling '*Dahng*'... MC at **Simon Cabaret**

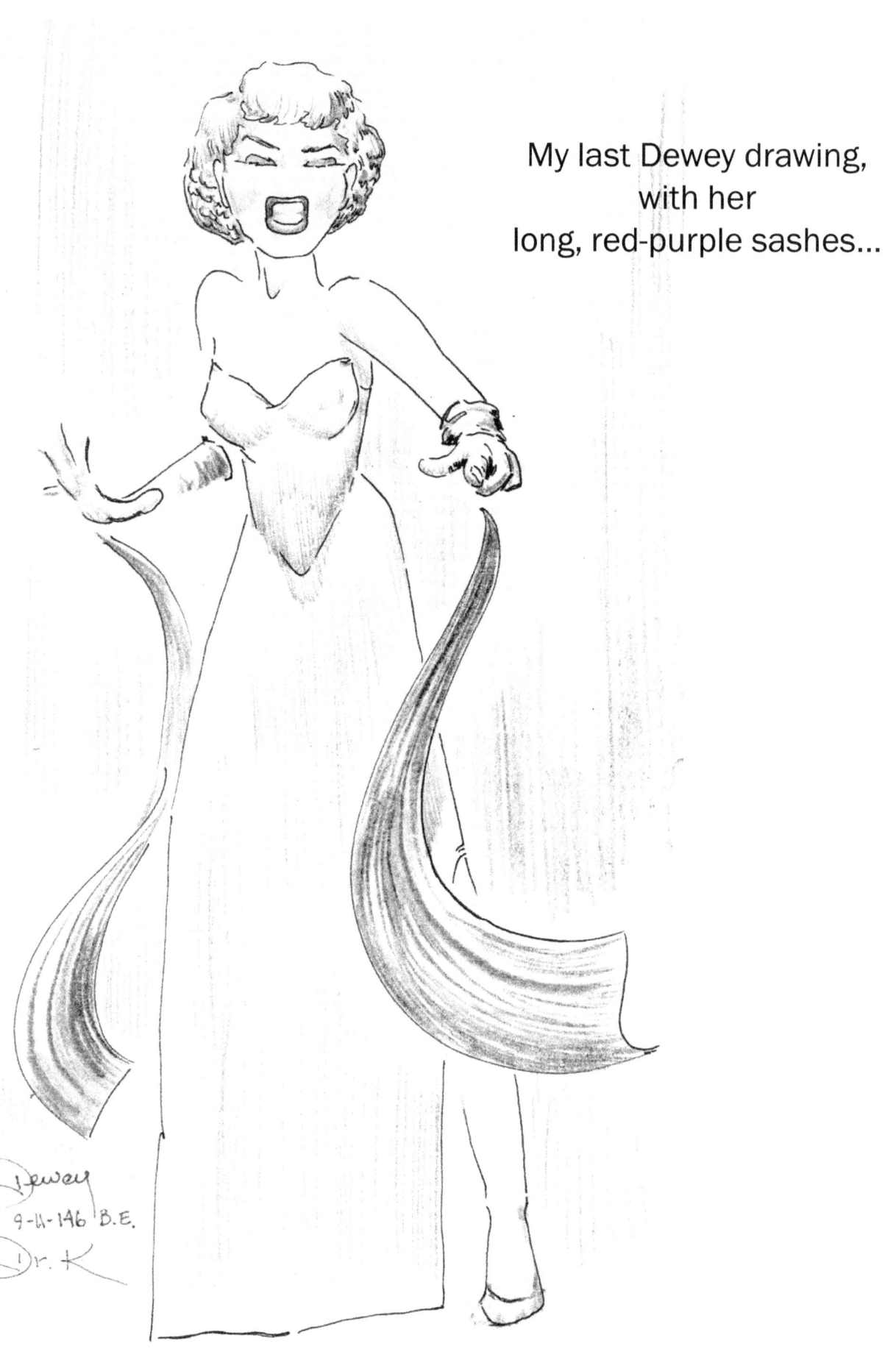

My last Dewey drawing,
with her
long, red-purple sashes...

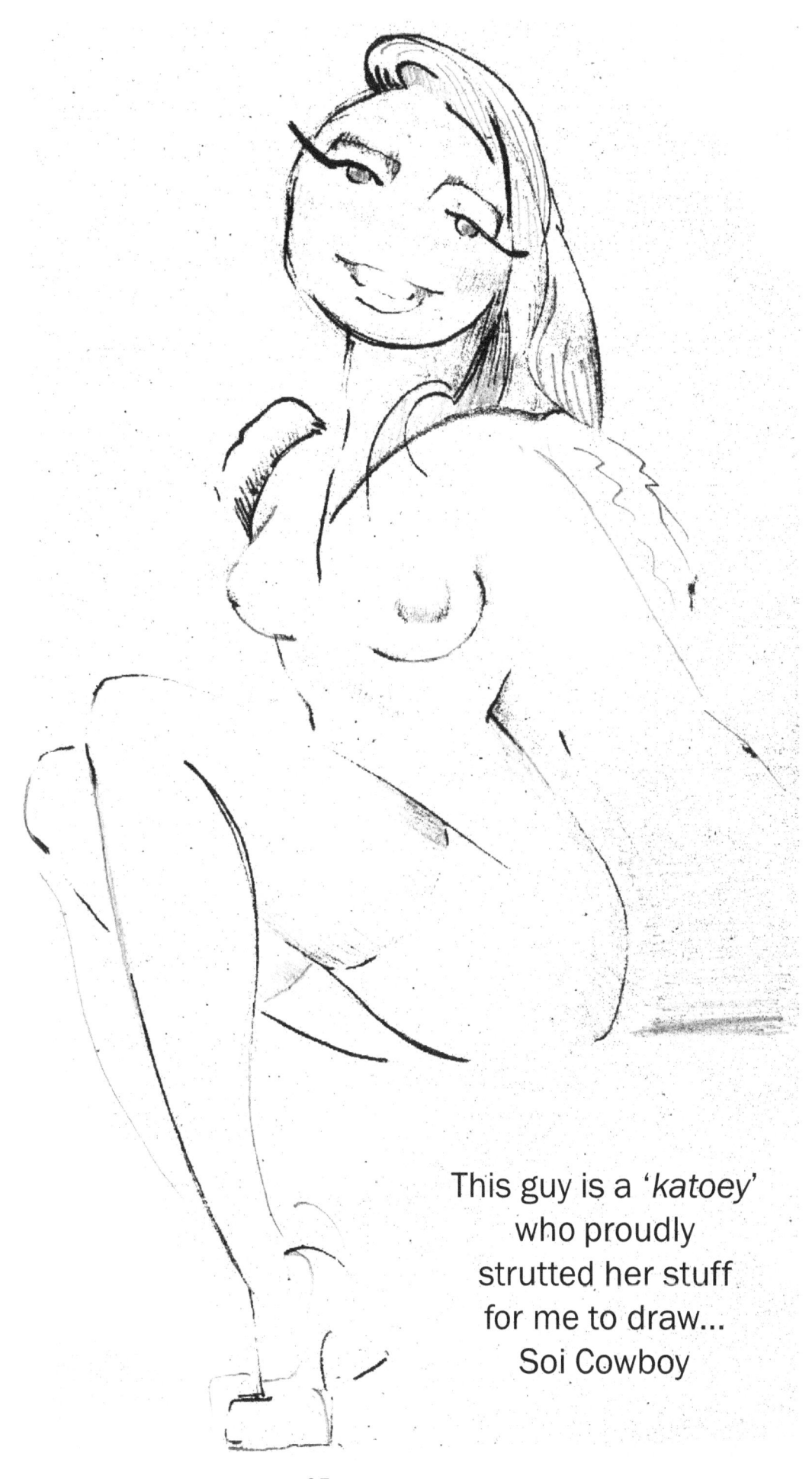

This guy is a 'katoey'
who proudly
strutted her stuff
for me to draw...
Soi Cowboy

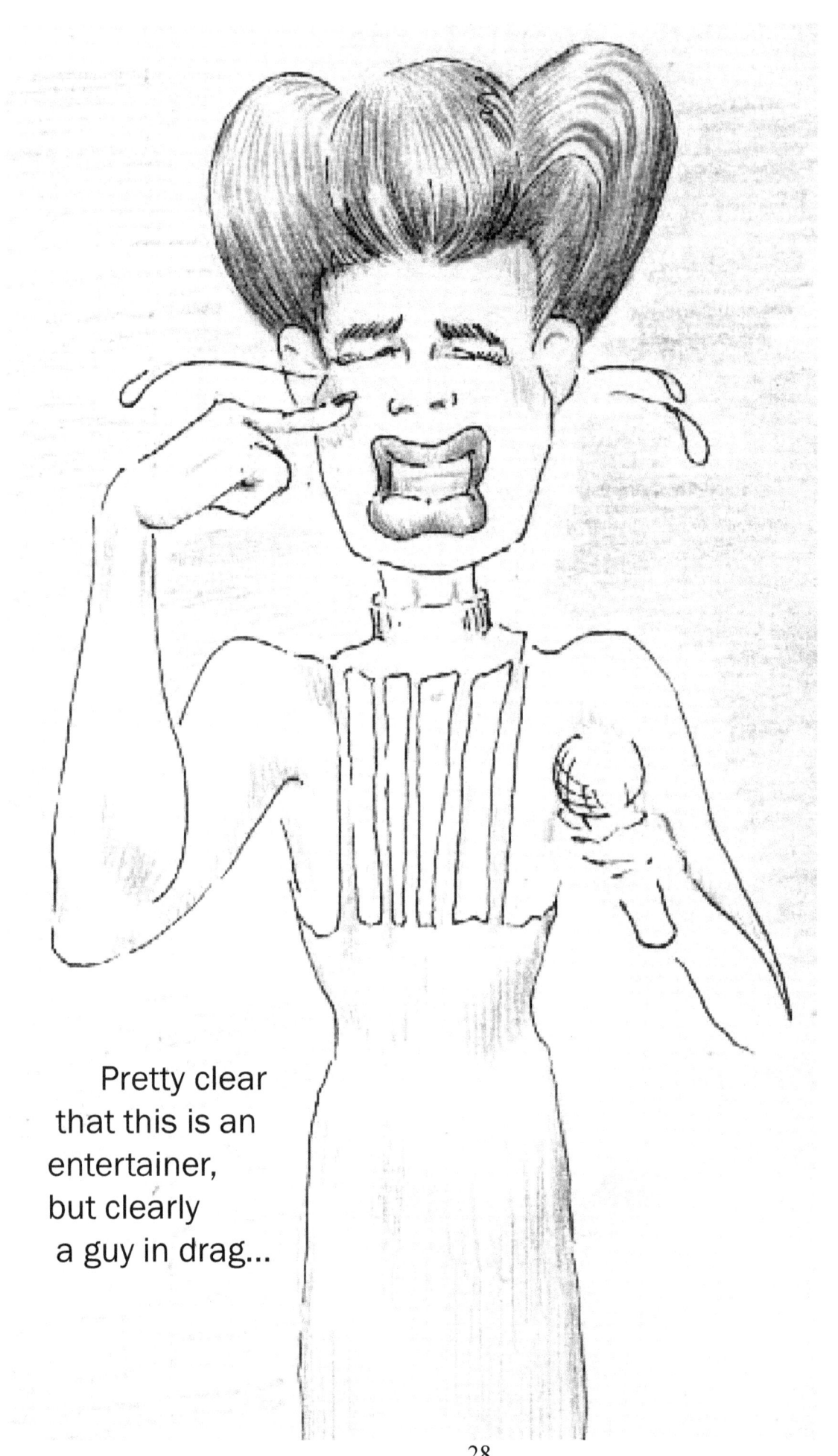

Pretty clear
that this is an
entertainer,
but clearly
a guy in drag...

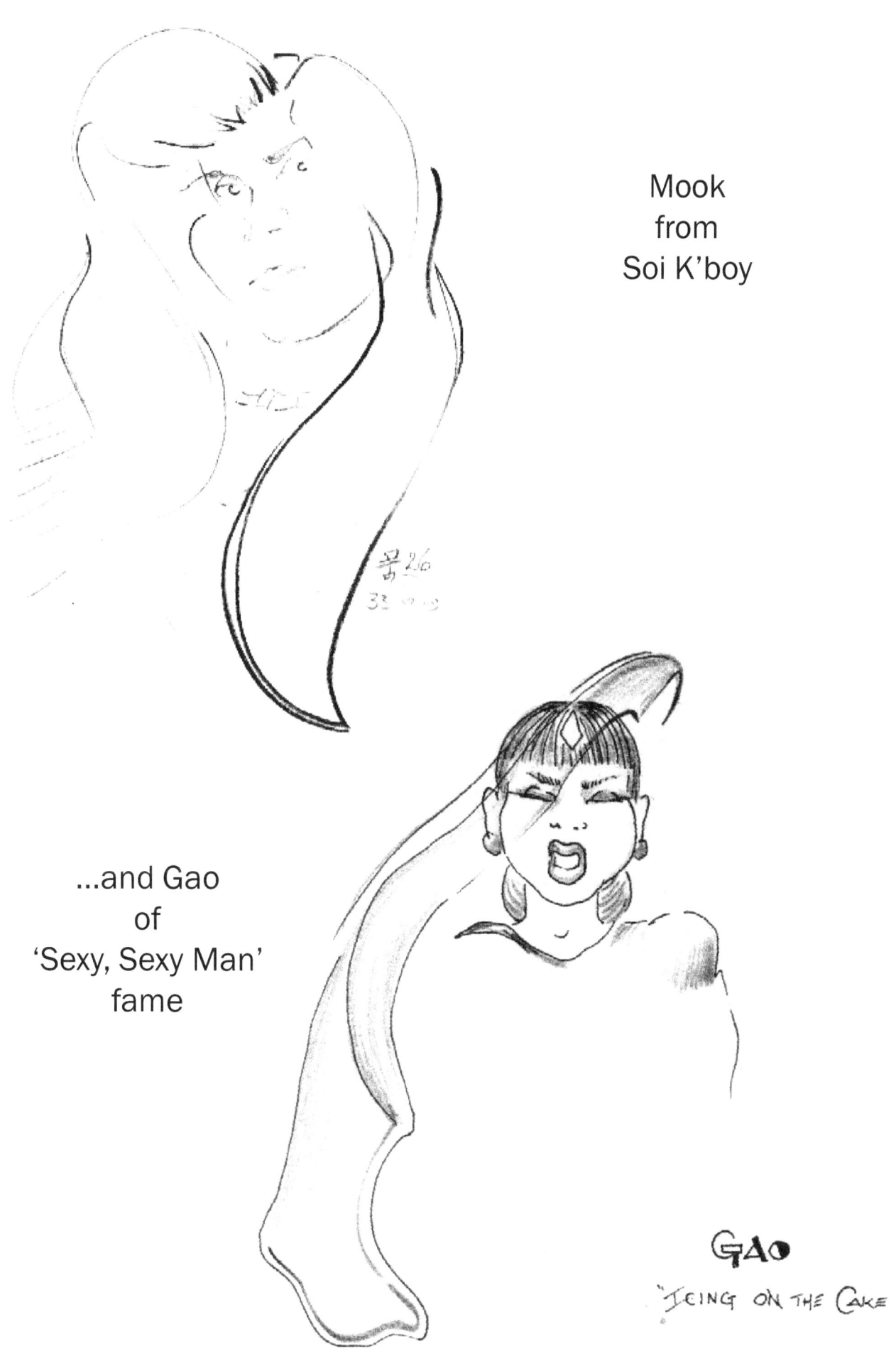

Mook
from
Soi K'boy

...and Gao
of
'Sexy, Sexy Man'
fame

GAO

"ICING ON THE CAKE

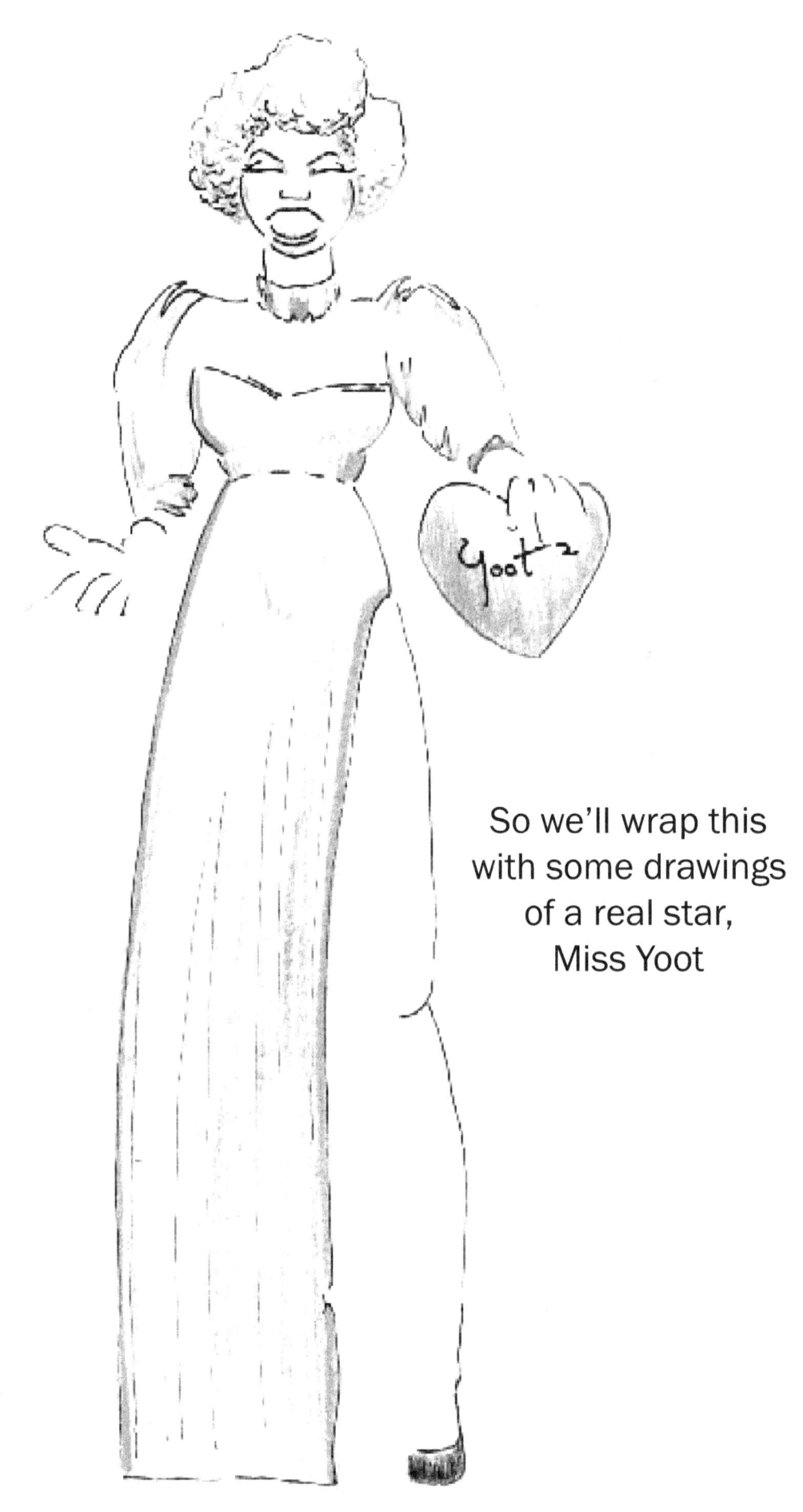

So we'll wrap this
with some drawings
of a real star,
Miss Yoot

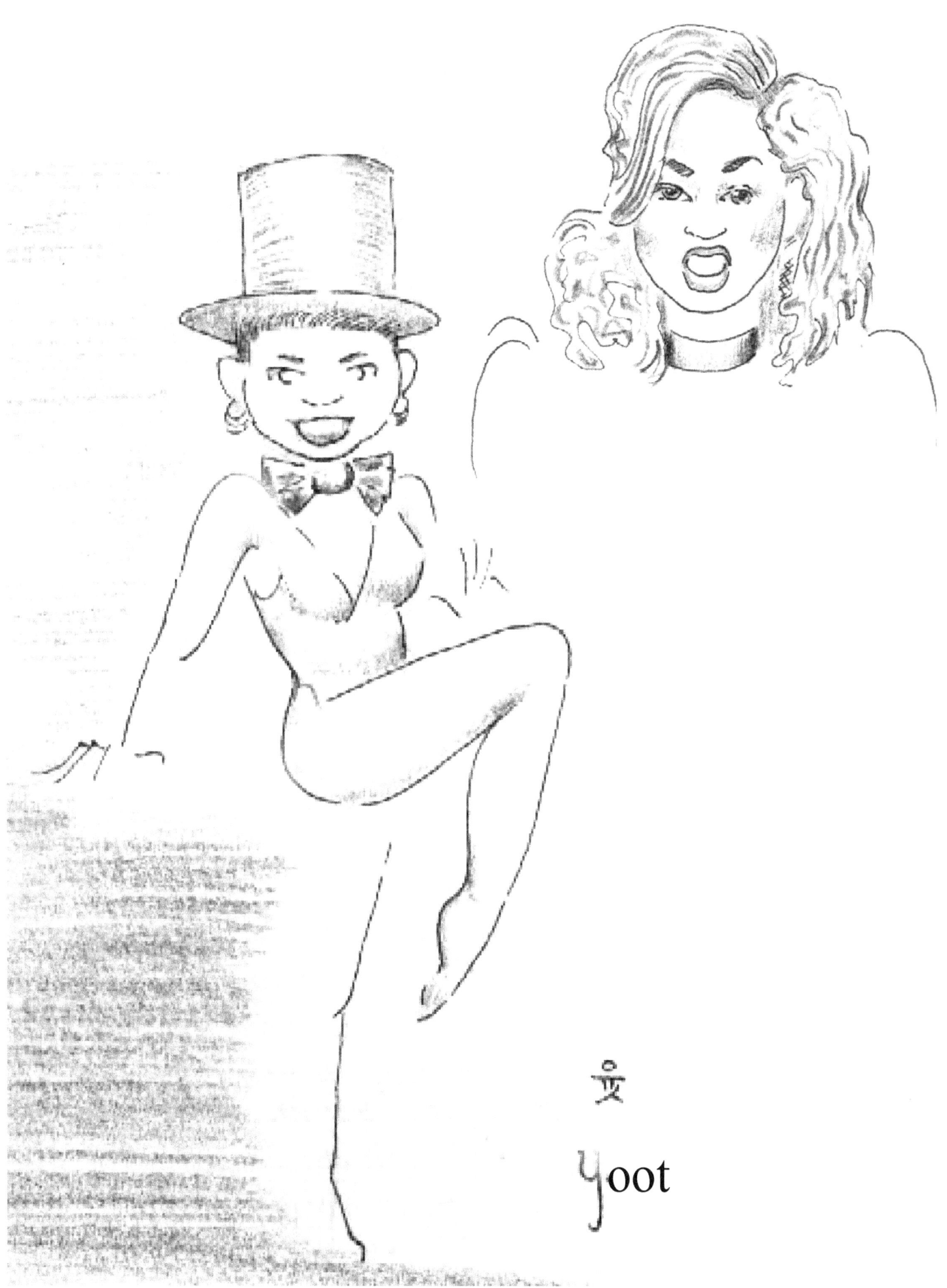

Yoot

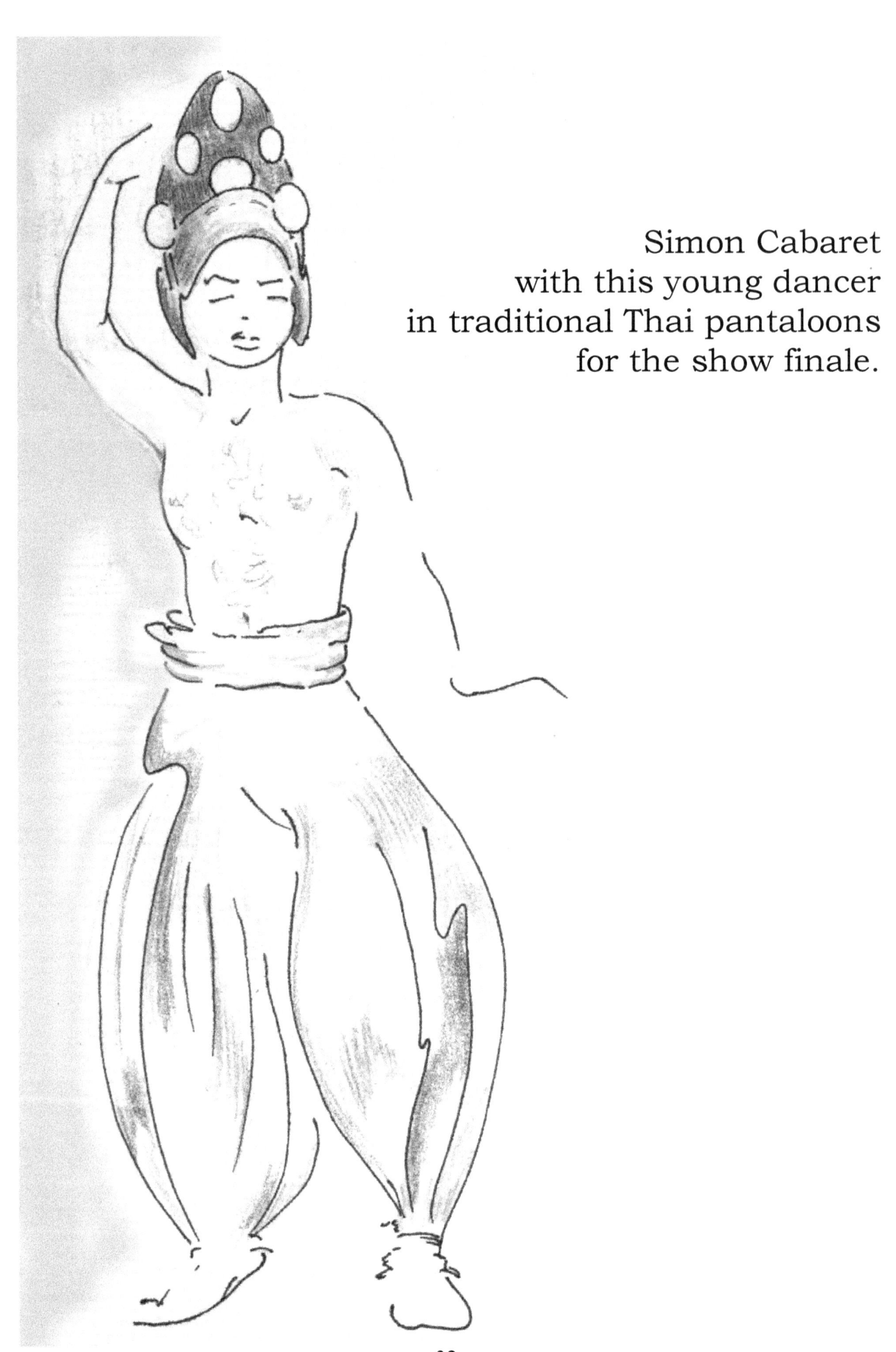

Simon Cabaret
with this young dancer
in traditional Thai pantaloons
for the show finale.

Trusting you enjoyed this 'Walk on the Wild Side'
and now you can just
Walk the Dinosaur
right on
outta here with Sid…

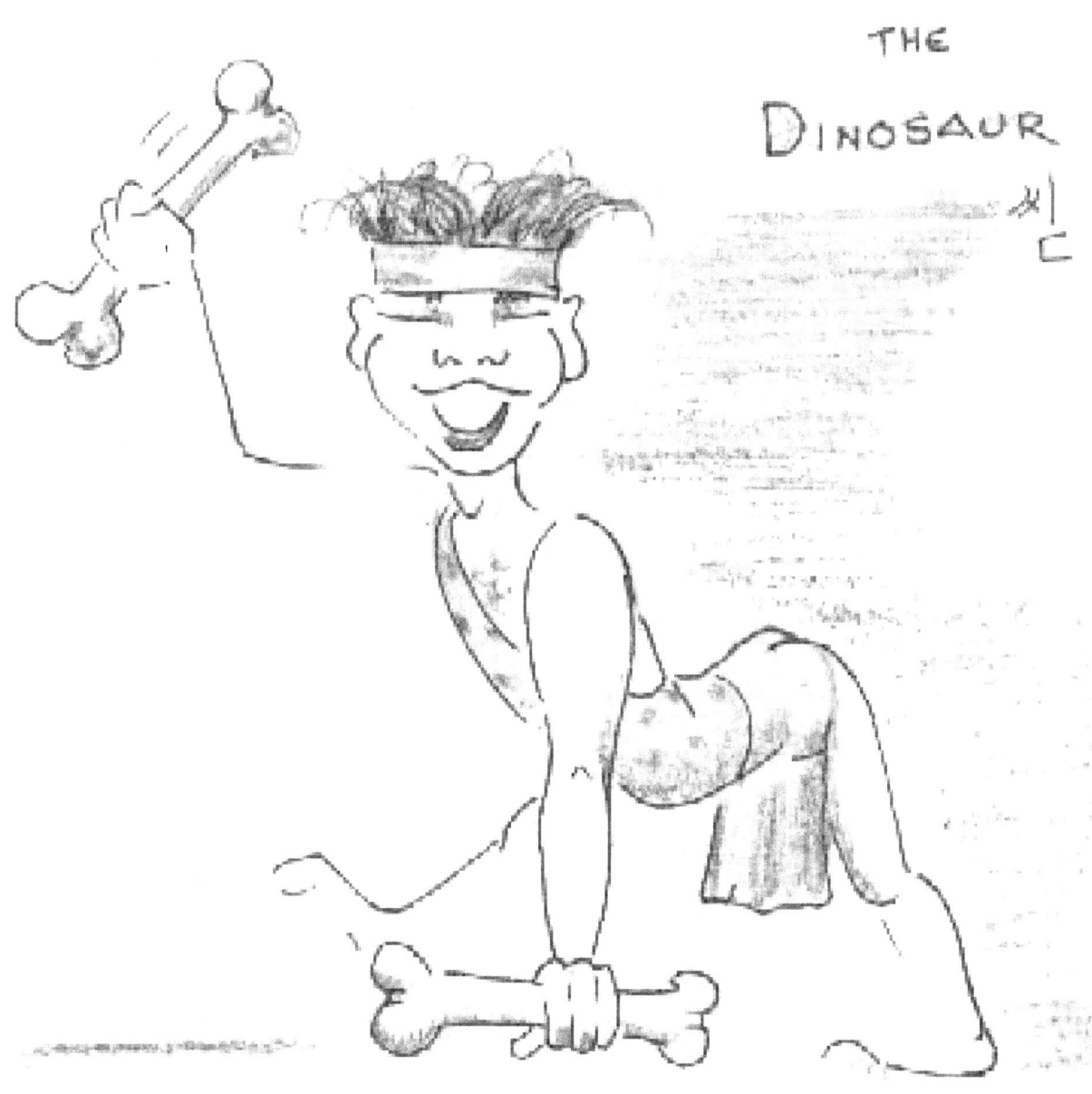

THE DINOSAUR

Appendix: After Words

-**Gaow** was a woman on the Simon Cabaret stage and team, and only reverted to soft-male after the shows ended and the lights went down. No surgery or chemo, he just enjoyed *dressing female* and dancing for good pay, in front of hundreds of tourists, nightly.

-Baby GoGo may have been Pattaya's most lucrative bar, but if so, it was in part because the owner sold SHARES at $10,000 a share; to Euro and Aussie and American investors... hundreds of them, until somebody got wise... the 'entertainers' were young teens, but they were ALL girls.

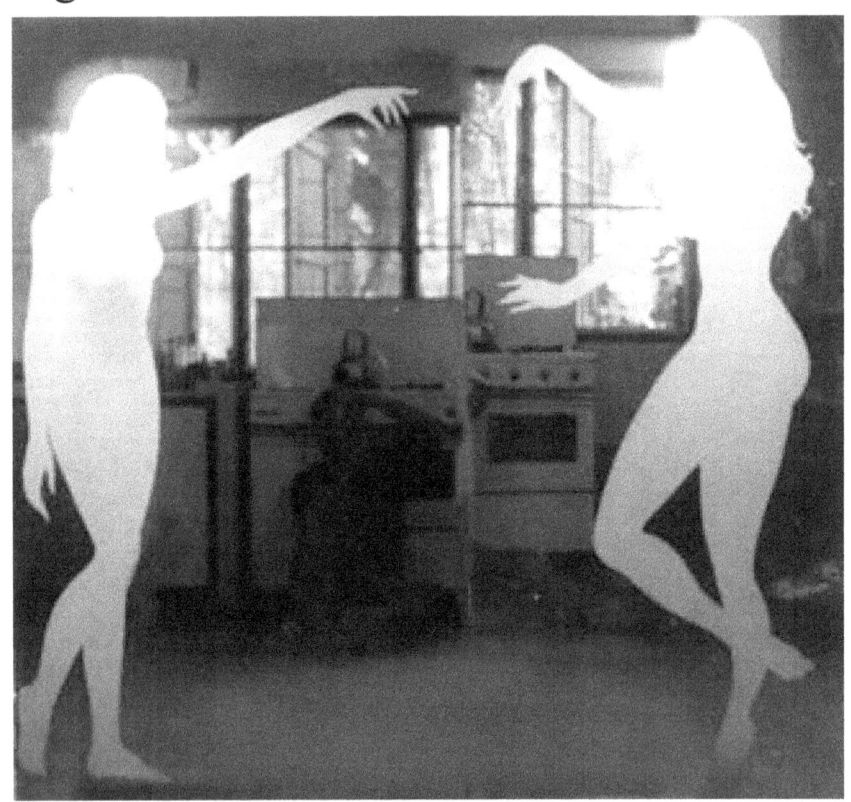

These are the mirrors I designed for Baby's interior. Gurls...

+Answer to a Frequently Asked Question: No, I did NOT 'sample the delights' of the ladies drawn and sketched here..

+Yes, some are *caricatures* and some are sketch-portraits.

+Page 4 **Eung** was one of my favorite subjects, as she had a lovely face, female figure (extensive, expensive surgery; daily chemo) and put in major hours every day practicing and polishing her steps, timing and lip-synch.

Moreover, she had a way of pulling her mouth into what was her trademark facial gesture. And since **Simon Cabaret** manager wanted to 'tease' the audience as much as possible, views of her cleavage were restricted to one (or rarely two) glimpses per show.

In any case, during the years I was drawing her, she got the finest costumes and most of the non-Tina Turner plum songs. She also played a co-starring role in a Hong Kong murder mystery, where she's a guy until the climactic final scenes and her non-male form is revealed. Can YOU find that online? circa 1987?

-Page 5 It's become a classic by now, so refresh your memory with Paul Anka's '**One Man Woman**' here, on YouTUBE:
        https://www.youtube.com/watch?v=sGZkdpgAoPc

This guy had it DOWN! Half of him was made up as a woman, and the other half made up and dressed as a man... even Chinese and Japanese tourists LOVED his performance, and he deserved the praise he garnered for a really professional act!

+Page 6 **Eung** again, in her emerald-and-ebony matador's outfit, doing a great performance at Simon Cabaret, South Pattaya. Her crowd-pleasing performances rocked the house!

-Page 7 Sam was one of the few manly, masculine performers at Simon Cabaret, and his 'Putting Out Fire' by David Bowie was an instant crowd-pleaser!

+Page 8 While Pattaya was in its post-Vietnam war/pre-Family era around 1980-2000, there were *katoeys* (Thai male homosexuals) there in Pattaya, and the TV-TS performers, but Pattaya was more generally targeted for the hetero male market. Still, the beach side of South Pattaya Road had **Simon Cabaret** and dozens of other shops and clubs, but only across the road from the beach was a small section of town for the visitors who wanted to 'Walk on the Wild Side' and that area was informally named 'Boys Town'.

The 'cabaret shows' were smaller (1.5 meters by 2 meters in the middle of the floor, no stage) and the calibre of 'entertainer' was much lower, to put it charitably. But some caught my eye, and I drew them.

-Page 9 Two more from Boys Town, and I should say that it was FORMALLY named such some years ago, and a big arch-sign was put up, because *not everybody* wanted to interact with TVs, TS or *katoeys*.

+Page 12 **Eung** here, in her scarlet-peach-plum outfit, dancing on the stage of Simon Cabaret.

-Page 13 **Eung** singing here under a pink-orange-yellow-plum headdress, and she had a good choreographer, too...

+Page 14 **Eung** in her scarlet-red dress-outfit, and she looked like dynamite! Fantastic!

-Page 15 **Chae** would show up once a night, wigged out and made up as Tina Turner, and lip-synched a crowd-clamoring chorus of - say- Tina's "You're the Best!" ... there were other Tinamatators, but Chae was the best!

+Page 16 **Chae** was the almost-as-starry as Eung, and possibly a bit more versatile than Eung, because Chae wasn't afraid of having physical action RUIN his investment in body sculpting.

-Page 17 **Chae** was so successful as Tina that I had to pick out only the best of the drawings for you, and made me wonder if there are any copyright infringement issues for a guy like **Chae**?

+Page 18 I think this is Chae, but it might have been one of the lesser stars, vamping to Eartha Kitt's 'Champagne Tastes'...

-Page 19 Now we come to Dewey... at least as talented as Chae, maybe even as overall brilliant as Eung, Dewey was a rather tall Thai who enjoyed getting paid to dress up as a woman and dance in front of hundreds of curious, international, paying customers!

+Page 20 Dewey dancing to Sade's **"Smooth Operator"**... don't know why, but Chinese tourists really DUG this one!

-Page 21 Dewey synching 'New York, New York!' . . colors here were a Brazilian Mardi Gras blare of orange and greens and pinks, but hey! New York it sang!

+Page 22 / 23 I was drawing Dewey in her silver-blue dress in an early-evening dress-rehearsal, when a woman walked up to my right, saw what I was doing, and said, "That's my brother..." and I didn't even look up, but corrected her, "You mean your sister..." but "No, he's my BROTHER!" she insisted, and I realized how far I'd fallen into the illusion, so I paused the Dewey-drawing and turned to do the near-portrait of Dewey's Sister, Page 23. She was proud of her brother, and she liked the drawings...

+Page 24 **Dewey** walking her stuff once again, this time in a much less gaudy 'New York, New York!' What color is THIS dress?

-Page 25 **Mr Dahng** was the MC at Simon Cabaret, as he had the best attitude and facial setup... all the show was pre-recorded in English, Chinese, Japanese, French... so he only had to lip-synch sort of, until he tossed a verbal bone to the Thais in the audience and behind the curtain... and he **was** capable in Thai!

+Page 26 **Dewey** here, but I didn't note the song in my sketch book, just the class, elegant impression that Dewey projected in motion or in stillness... he was a lovely, charming woman when he wanted to be.

-Page 27 And again, know that the word '*katoey*' is a socially-acceptable word for 'effeminate male' or 'male homosexual'. And this *katoey* KNEW he had a fine, feminine body, and flaunted it for my fast-scratching pen!

+Page 28 One of the B-grade *katoeys* from Boys Town, doing some weepy, tearful lip-synch, all while radiating a 'guy in drag' vibe...

-Page 29 (Top) **Mook**, from Soi K'boy (Sukumwit Soi 23) was working freelance outside several of the nightclubs of this hetero male nightspot.

(bottom right) Gao (or Gaow) you met earlier in this coloring book. He was physically small, and had a real knack for dressing like and IMITATING women... which was 'Icing On the Cake'

+Page 30/31 **Yoot** comes in here, to grace these last pages with the brightness of her smile, and the swagger of his strut! Radiating male or female, on different days, seemed to be well within his power, at the flick of a swish!

And with our final two pages going to the Guys of Simon Cabaret, here are 'Thai Traditional Mens' Wear' and Sid, doing his version of 'Walk the Dinosaur'

I hope you've enjoyed coloring these, as much as I have enjoyed drawing them, which was tiny compared to the joy and insights I gleaned by meeting them, speaking Thai with them, *listening* Thai to their tribulations, tests and triumphs, and I look forward to your comments and feedback as you email Info@TeamWorx-Inc.com

If you want more like this, say so. If you find this objectionable in some way, tell me why. If you have a special set of drawings you'd like, tell me, but please understand I have always done erotic, never porn, and have NO INTENTION of changing this.

Yeah, I've lost some big contracts for being a prude like this, but I've sone some other carved-glass works that were erotic, lovely and the kind of beauty I'd show my grandmother... or yours! With pride!

So again, I've enjoyed making these books for you, and am grateful that good people like you buy 3-4 copies for your friends and enemies.

Karridine

Karridine

People Dreams #4:
Trannies, TVs & Entertainers
An Adult Coloring Book

Rated PG (Parental Guidance)... this is *almost* family suitable, but since it does show professional dancers in various lovely stages of undress, it is probably NSFW.

And the subject matter is TransVestites, Transgenders and homo-sexual cabaret entertainers, so use wisdom in who you share this with.

So enjoy the subtle and overt pleasures of the human female form, in born-females and tuck-n-roll chemo-surgical wunderkind, as you add color and details to these line-drawings, pen-and-inks, done on-location in Pattaya and Bangkok, Thailand, by artist Karridine.

These are some of the faces and forms who danced across the life-path of Karridine, and now grace the pages of this coloring book.

For further info on carved-glass custom designs, or to order your lover's portrait in glass or mirror, contact
Karridine (at) **Gmail.com**

For a chance to help make the indie film 'Cleanup Crew', go to
http://bit.ly/1HCuLk9

www.ingramcontent.com/pod-product-compliance
Lightning Source LLC
Chambersburg PA
CBHW080652180526

45168CB00008B/3397